PRAISE FOR

Blossom: The Wild Ambassador Of Tewksbury

"This unusual tribute to a wild deer surpasses expectations. Unique for its gripping plot and smoldering spotlight on the brutality of hunting these living, breathing fauna, the book compares to no other."

—BookLife Prize Critique / Publisher's Weekly

"In riveting detail ... with the tension of a thriller .... A thought-provoking, poignant, and unusual love story that lingers."

—Kirkus Reviews

"Simply and eloquently written ... Blossom's extraordinary story defies traditionally held beliefs regarding the divide between man and nature and is likely to cause readers to reassess their assumptions about 'wild' animals. It is sure to appeal to anyone who savors the beauty of our natural world."

—BlueInk Review - *Notable Book Award

"A gorgeous interplay of images and words that will keep readers engaged, engrossed, and educated about the plight of wildlife in growing human habitats and deer in particular."

—Midwest Book Review - D. Donovan, Senior Reviewer

"Carner brings wonderful animal energy to her writing … adds movement and flavor to all the sensory triumph in this book. We experience its sense of place, its natural beauty."

—Writer's Digest

"A beautiful memoir of healing and hope wrapped up in the story of how one helpless fawn found both."

—Chanticleer Int'l Book Reviews "Best Book"

"This lovely story, told with heart and candor, demonstrates how we share our lives with all beings on this planet. Read this book and experience the joy and surprise of the life of Blossom, a most amazing deer."

—Georgia Hughes, Editor, former bookseller

"*Blossom: the Wild Ambassador of Tewksbury*, is to twenty-first century wildlife what Felix Salten's *Bambi, a Life in the Woods*, was to wildlife a century ago. The vital connection between humans and our animal cousins is revived in Anna Carner's compelling, heartfelt memoir."

—Ron Maxwell, writer-director of *Gettysburg, Gods and Generals*, and *Copperhead*

Blossom: The Wild Ambassador of Tewksbury

The True Story Of A Wild Deer
With An Amazing Personality

ANNA CARNER

WITH POEMS BY

JEANNE HAMILTON TROAST

Sibylline
DIGITAL FIRST

Sibylline
Press

For Pino

This book is dedicated with all my heart to my husband, Pino Blangiforti, who held my hand, and encouraged me to dance amongst the stars in my sky.

Contents

Prologue

As animal lovers, we believe in the power of words to open minds, touch hearts, and inspire action against deliberate cruelty.

More than a story, this is a journey of an extraordinary bond between Blossom, an orphaned fawn, and Anna, a woman grappling with childhood trauma. Their unique friendship, filled with joy and fear, will tug at your heartstrings and deepen your appreciation for nature's wonders and the power of compassion. Blossom, the only wild animal ever nominated for Purina's Pet of the Year award, became a symbol of hope. Her story, featured in National Geographic's "The Private Life of Deer," sparked a significant shift in perspectives on hunting and gun laws in rural communities, inspiring many to reconsider their stance on animal welfare.

Once reluctant to engage in conflict, Anna cannot ignore Blossom's plight. She uses her paramedic skills to save Blossom, but in a beautiful twist, Blossom also saves Anna, leading her on a path of self-discovery and growth.

Their friendship, a beacon of hope and resilience, is a testament to the enduring power of love and compassion.

Thoughts

My memories are mine alone. They are undoubtedly embellished over time, but not fabricated. Some names, scenes, and characteristics have been altered to respect the privacy of individuals. I apologize to anybody I left out or if time-compressed sequences don't match your recollections.

But Blossom's essence is here within these pages. For those of you who knew her, I ask you to dwell upon a moment when you were in the right spot, at the right time, and a 'wild' deer kissed you and captured your heart.

Nonfiction writing demands personal risk-taking and, ultimately, catharsis. What I did not expect, nor welcome at first, was this story's insistence on chipping away at sealed-over conflicts and trauma from my childhood.

"Be brave," people told me. But I was not brave enough until Blossom provided the incentive.

—Anna Carner

For Blossom

I wonder if I have lived before; ever
passed through this world as someone
less or more? Ever tried
with all my heart to be someone
more than what you see?

Could I have been no one at all?
Perhaps, a leaf about to fall
or even sweeter still, a bird by
whose song your heart was stirred.

And what of you while I was another?
Were you my sister or a brother? Could
you have been a rose about to flower,
and I the sun or April shower?
Would I have known in all these stages,
how dear you'd be, if
I was you and you were me? Alas,

my memory's weak, it's hard to remember
what happened last week, forget September.
There is one thing of which I'm sure,
on which I'd stake a lifetime's wages.
You were loved through all my ages.

— Jeanne Hamilton Troast

Chapter 1

Unicorn Hollow

Spring— May 26, 1999

Secure in the warmth of my horse's body, I leaned over his neck and gave a gentle tug on his mane.

"*Tchk tchk* ... let's go, Justinian."

We were in the groove of the new day and blended with a spectacular landscape where songbirds chatted beneath cornflower-blue skies and morning haze swirled like spun sugar through rows of corn at the bottom of historic Fox Hill Road. Even the rolling buzz of empty-bellied bees in search of sweet nectar sounded muffled.

Quietly alert, a family of deer watched our progress from the edge of the field. I grinned at the playful awkwardness of a couple of long-legged fawns vying for the attention of a mature buck. He stood tall and vigilant, dark eyes missing nothing, snorted a small alarm, and stomped his foot. In one intuitive swoop, four flared white plumes and two slender feather-like tails played catch-up into the trees and out of sight.

Life was there for all to enjoy, except, of course, if you lived life as a target.

The earth smelled clean and alive. Vintage Tewksbury.

My saddle squeaked with the sounds of well-cared-for leather as I urged my horse near the trunk of a gnarly old tree loaded with floral rosettes, the first in a long row hugging the southern slope of the old orchard. The rich, musky aroma of damp earth mingled with a slight scent of apple blossoms.

Feeling the moment, I opened my arms wide and blew a kiss into the bright morning sky.

"Want an apple, Justinian?" I reached into the leather pouch clipped across the back of my saddle. "Yummy. Da-licious. Bet you didn't know eating two apples a day is like brushing twice? It's nature's toothbrush. Trust me. Here." I stretched across his white mane. Justinian turned toward me, nickered, and took a three-quarters bite of the apple I held out.

"Hey, don't be oinkish."

I ate what was left, picked up the reins, and signaled my Arabian into a smooth canter toward home.

In a little more than half an hour, we were trotting under a dense canopy of oaks bordering the small farm we called Unicorn Hollow. I dismounted and led Justinian across the narrow bridge. It rained the night before—a soft spring rain, and I listened as our temperamental stream surged into a gurgling current over the rocks below. Timid by nature, Justinian was worried but followed.

I unlatched and pushed open the gates. Five white pear trees edged the blacktop driveway leading to our red gambrel-roofed barn, only fifty feet from the road. The weathered wood was wet and darker today, in contrast to the barrels of salmon-colored geraniums around its perimeter. The barn had a hayloft, four stalls, a washing area, and a tack room.

By the time I untacked, washed, and brushed Justinian, the air felt thick and damp. I opened the stall to the grassiest paddock, where our other two horses were grazing. Justinian whinnied and trotted toward them.

★ ★ ★

The front of our house snugged into the slope of a hill in Tewksbury, New Jersey. Horse country—within the mini-boundaries between what passed for the rural wilderness and the more suburban "commuter" towns, an hour west of New York City.

We'd wanted to live in Tewksbury for years; I'd longed for a barn—my husband, Pino, had his heart set on a vegetable garden. One day, a "wrong" turn up a hill, a scenic view, and horseback riders in the street led us to the home we would buy a year later.

It needed work, but so what? The setting was perfect.

The low-profile ranch fronted the woods across Wildwood Road, dipping dramatically in the back along the roll of Fox Hill Road toward Oldwick. The real charm and pizzazz began with the view from the back wall of windows that allowed us to watch our animals closely in the countryside's serene, ever-changing color palette. Soft paisley summer greens turned into the crimson brilliance of autumn, then to winter's stark gray and white shades.

I heard our Maltese pup, Kaya, yip as she raced down the lawn toward me. Pino must have let her out. I didn't see him on the patio but waved anyway.

"Silly girl. Come with me." I walked the fence line to check out what might have been a cracked board. Kaya was full of fun and courage, all eight pounds of her. She skittered through rotting debris and new vegetation in places I would have negotiated only with boots and a stick.

"Oops!" I said as she tripped, rolled, and continued to traipse around the hardwoods and bushes bordering the stream.

A quiver of motion at the edge of an old yellow forsythia caught my eye. The flutter of nesting chickadees sounded like a mini-military honor guard, a warning of sorts.

I jogged toward Kaya, laughing at the way our lovable pup bounced through the tall switch grass—ears flapping, tail wagging—a come-to-life ping pong ball—full of joy. She spotted something and stood her ground, barking.

"Now what?" I wondered.

I got close enough to see a tunnel-like hole punched through the grass. A good-sized stick was nearby, which I grabbed, tense and prepared, in case of snakes.

I hate snakes.

"Kaya, what is it?" I began to imagine other things—creatures stirring, ready to strike at my little dog. She was easy prey for aggressive animals, even large birds. It was not a comforting thought that her only defense was me.

"Come here, NOW!" She didn't listen, unusual behavior for her. I tried to see, then tentatively moved forward, reached out, and parted the tall grass with the stick.

I gasped in surprise. "Oh, my God!"

"*Aehh* ..." A small fawn's soft cry of distress sounded like mewing from a kitten.

So tender and tiny, the baby lay flat on a patch of matted grasses, as if someone forgotten—head arched, legs stiff and straight, almost lifeless—the little mouth fixed open in a mock cry, taut edges curled, straining to breathe. Under a blanket of dew, her polka-dotted skin appeared stretched tight over fragile bones, while the hollow beneath her ribs jumped in time with her heart.

"Oh, no, baby," I cooed and knelt to cup her damp chest and rump with my hands. The chilly night had drained the warmth from her. The most obvious threat to her survival was dehydration and exposure.

She exhaled a weak puff of air.

"Careful, Kaya!" She continued to sniff at the petite black feet, her tail wagging nonstop at her find.

Where was the fawn's mother? I scanned the fields to the tree line, hoping for a glimpse of the doe. Disappointed but not surprised, I saw no one.

She was perhaps only a few days old—and she was dying.

I recalled the stark warnings from a local magazine: "Never interfere with a downed wild animal, not even a newborn! Diseases, insects—there's no telling what dangers lurk nearby, waiting to latch onto an unsuspecting passerby. You'll drive off its mother; she'll abandon her baby if she detects the scent of a human."

"*Aehh ... aehh ...*" As if her tiny heart were breaking, the fawn called for her mother, again and again. Another dog barked from somewhere.

The fawn's ears twitched, and big eyes opened, wide with fear. I lifted her head. Suddenly, she stared at me, at first in terror, and then with soft, pleading eyes.

This baby would not survive.

In the early 80s, I was a paramedic in Miami. Now, I pushed myself into a calming routine—my training turned on the gears in my mind and fingers, searching for the protocol to save her life. "Where's your mama?" I tried to comfort her with gentle whispers and humming. "Let's take a peek at you." She allowed my soft prodding.

I felt no bumps, abnormalities, or tenderness along her spine or bones. Pale gums and rapid breathing were sure signs of shock. What was I not seeing?

I remembered what Captain Randy reminded me of in paramedic class: "Anna, stay calm—assess your patient first, then verify." The ABCs of life are: Airway open—check; breathing—check; circulation—check. "Remember, shock kills. Move fast but efficiently, and remember that the most visible injuries may not be the worst."

I put my finger in her mouth. She weakly sucked on it.

I slid my arms under her shoulders, neck, and backside, balanced her head in the crook of my arm, and scooped her off the ground. She weighed only a few pounds, as light as a bundle of feathers. I held her limp body close to my chest for warmth and turned toward the house. I felt her tremble, and her long legs dangled at my sides.

I didn't know about the language or sounds of deer then, so I cooed to her in soft, mellow tones and hums our mama alpacas used with their babies—soothing chatter, probably more comforting to me than the fawn.

"Live, little girl. You can do it."

When I hurried through the old barn paddock, Justinian started toward me, his silver-white tail swishing from side to side and his bright white body reflecting the sun. He stopped to watch.

"Not now, boy." He appeared puzzled.

One more gate to open—single-handed. I slipped through the area where a few alpaca females were resting on the lawn with their babies on the steep rise behind the house.

I was out of breath and only halfway there when a flurry of gunshots boomed and echoed against the hills, like roiling clouds building on the edge of a thunderstorm.

"Ugh!" I jumped and realized the likely fate of the fawn's mother.

I rested my hand on the pitifully sick animal. If she lived, would she be safe here?

Don't think about it.

Chapter 2

The Fawn

The drama unfolding in the field below must have caught Pino's attention because he opened the patio door, voice urgent. "What's wrong?"

I paused for breath and repositioned the baby's head in the crook of my arm as my husband traversed the slope toward me, appearing more like a sprinter than a New York corporate-type turned farmer.

"How bad?" he asked and bent over the shivering fawn.

"Bad."

"I'll grab some supplies from the alpaca shed," he said. "Check the levels of oxygen in the tank, bring a bag of Lactated Ringer's solution and new IV tubing. I'll set her up in the house, okay?"

His large hand rested on the small animal for a few seconds, and then he was off at a run.

I took the shortcut through our office and carried the fawn upstairs to a bathroom we used when a newborn alpaca needed extra medical attention.

The baby deer flopped like an old Raggedy Ann doll on a thick bathmat in the corner of the glassed-in shower. I switched on the infrared ceiling lamp and grabbed a towel. Pino bought me an electronic stethoscope last Christmas. It was in the bathroom cabinet with an assortment of supplies we needed for emergencies.

"*Aehh … aehh …*" The fawn cried—long, drawn-out, high-pitched piteous wailing.

I was stunned at the depth of her grief. Just like a person. I didn't realize … I never thought about it.

She grunted when her head flipped over her spotted back and stayed there. Like touching a breakable doll, I carefully brought it forward on the mat.

She shivered.

A seismic rumble of early memories blurred into a gut-wrenching ache: being carried as my mother screamed, my sister Mary cried, and I desperately tried to squirm out from under the suffocating cloak of chaos and pain.

It was as if she were me; I knew the fawn's anguish and thought back to a time when I was a child alone in the hospital, filled with fear and bewilderment—begging for all to be made right again. I had almost forgotten.

Stop it! Don't go there!

I tried to soothe the tiny deer. "Okay, baby … shhh …" Her ear rotated toward me. She stopped crying.

She was listening.

All became still—too still. "NO!"

The fawn's eyes rolled back. Her tongue drooped between her lips.

Where was the next breath? Her chest was still.

I rubbed the little body and tried to visualize her heart, lungs, and breathing. My scope picked up an erratic heartbeat. Not great, but she wasn't dead either. Although her cardiac rhythm was abnormal and her pulse weak, her heart sounds were crisp—no noticeable whooshing or arrhythmias.

Her lack of responsiveness scared me more than anything.

Traumatic shock can prevent oxygenation in the brain; blood pressure drops and causes a shutdown of the lungs and organs. Just like a mechanical engine, the whole system continues to spiral down, finally quitting.

"Let's try this, baby." I massaged her, hoping the added stimulus would invigorate her sluggish cardio-vascular system. "You can do it ... come on." I increased the pressure, using longer, pulling strokes. Open hands, one under her body, one over, kneading her flaccid muscles, from neck to tail and down her legs, hoping to raise her blood pressure.

She flicked her tail.

"What the —?" I hadn't noticed a slight movement of something on her rear end before. I raised her tail by the white-tipped end with stomach-squeezing disgust.

Damn, maggots! I hated those opportunistic parasites, those disgusting creepy crawlies that showed up to feed on death. I searched the medicine cabinet and found half a bottle of soapy antiseptic.

"Say goodbye, bugs!" I muttered under my breath and started the dirty job. I cleaned the parasites off with gauze pads dunked in the solution, followed by a soothing antiseptic ointment. The parasites wouldn't have the meal they were hoping for today. This was war on a microscopic level, and I was determined to win. She remained still through it all.

"Whew!" Pino grunted as he hauled the oxygen tank up the stairs on its chunky wheels. "Full." He set the unit outside the door and opened the flow-valve. "Is she still alive?"

"She's in shock. Heart's erratic—thought she wouldn't make it once."

I eased my pinky finger into her mouth to keep it open and placed the soft baby-sized oxygen mask over her face. Once again, her head swung back and needed to be flexed forward to allow an open airway. I rested her head in the palm of my hand.

Suddenly, she inhaled a shuddering gulp of air—her heart and lungs battling for the number one essential ingredient for life—oxygen.

"If she goes into cardiac arrest, how the heck will I manage CPR?" I worried.

"Is CPR possible on an animal? No way! How are you going to put your mouth around her face? Besides ..." Pino persisted, "... it's not clean!"

"Anything's possible," I pushed back, cocking my head and shifting my jaw for a better feel of how to make my idea work. "I'll have to try, though, won't I?"

"Your mouth over her mouth and nose?" He was serious, but the way he screwed up his face was full of good humor. "I'll get a washcloth. You're gonna need it!"

I hung the bag of Ringer's on a loop of twine around the shower head and let the tube and catheter hang free.

"Uh-oh!" The bag was cool. "Hey, sweetness," I called after him. "Bring me a pail of hot water." The subcutaneous drip of replacement body fluids should not enter her body cool; it would drop her temperature to dangerously low levels. The technique I liked best worked well to regulate body temperature and was simple, even on cold nights in the barn.

"Careful." Pino returned with the steaming pail and washcloth. I coiled a yard of surgical tubing and dropped it into the hot water. The liquid warmed within minutes.

"Okay, here we go. Thanks. Love you." I smiled at him, then advanced the needle under the fawn's belly skin. I opened the volume slide on the tube.

She was not quite dead, yet not exactly alive either.

The large, flat, metallic shower head shimmered in the red glow of the heat lamp, dangling clear plastic tubes of life-giving fluids into the baby resting below. She lay on her side, exhausted, looking like a puppet, whimsical behind the plastic oxygen mask with a painted-on smiley face. As she shifted her head, the mask moved, like a cartoon character come to life.

The baby deer jockeyed in and out of consciousness for several hours. My stethoscope told the story of a body in recovery as clearly as any visual screening. Her temperature climbed toward normal, for a baby alpaca, anyway.

I had fallen asleep against the wall, my hand still resting on the fawn's slender back legs. Pino shook my shoulder. "You have to eat something. I'll heat some soup." So very Italian. "Should I get your back brace?" I warmed to the concern in his voice.

"Thanks. Ouchy." The year before, I had ruptured a disk in my lower back. I stretched and adjusted the earpieces of my stethoscope. "Be there in a minute. What kind of soup?"

"Chicken barley," he said.

I could taste it already. Pino's comfort food always made the day better.

"Lungs sound clear." I sat up and shut my eyes to concentrate. "No abnormal beats now, her heart is steadier." Good. I flipped the scope around my neck.

A few drops of water every so often on her tongue with an eyedropper was the best way to keep her mouth moist under the oxygen mask. Later, I decided to coat my finger with pure honey and offered the sleepy baby with what I thought was a healthy sugar boost. She raised her head, flicked her tongue out, and curled it up on the sides, like a little scooper.

"Whoa! Where did that come from?" Strange, all this action in her neck and head while the rest of her body remained so still. A disconnect in motion was an ominous sign—she might have spinal cord damage—an impossible situation for an animal trying to survive in the wild.

"Will she make it?" Pino asked.

"Don't know."

Kaya waited with us, sniffling at the tiny, black, cloven feet.

It was one of those quiet, cozy times when whispers and tip-toes replaced the frenzied sounds of a medical emergency. After the rush of doing what needed to be done, and the beginning of the wait for the body to take over and heal itself. I stroked the fawn's silky fur while we helped her try to live, adjusting her body position every so often to prevent fluid buildup in her lungs. Hours later, she yawned and stiffened into a prolonged shuddering stretch.

"Look, Pino, she's watching us." Beautiful brown eyes—searching eyes—started to follow the action in the room. I expected a measure of panic, but her demeanor showed no evidence of terror.

As she rested on the edge of awareness, her ears rotated toward the quiet sounds around her, reminiscent of large satellite dishes searching for answers in the universe. I removed the catheter from her side and let the mask rest near her nose, still adding oxygen to the air. She breathed, even and steady.

I kissed her just beneath the ear, then softly traced my fingers down her legs to her tiny, pointy, patent-leather-looking feet. Twinkle toes.

The fawn's eyes half-opened in response, and she sighed with a squeak. Content, she fell back into a deep sleep.

"Yes!" I gave the closed-fist arm pump like my son Glen uses when something good happens. "Hang in there, sweet baby."

All became silent, except for the soft hiss of air flowing from the oxygen tank.

Chapter 3

A Lifetime Ago

An hour passed, possibly more. A cozy stillness enveloped the room, subdued in the ambient mid-afternoon light.

Every so often, the fawn mouth-breathed with disquieting squeaks, pops, and flutters from her lungs.

I waited, motionless, and gazed at her—perfect legs tucked up close beneath her belly on the bathmat in the shower stall, her body curled, nose to tail. I wondered about the visceral tug of tenderness and the crossroads of events that brought us together, even imagining a fantasy future with a fawn as a friend.

Click-whoosh ... click-whoosh ... click-whoosh ... The hiss of flowing oxygen and the mesmerizing cadence of an air clack valve pulled me into dreamlike equilibrium, to a snippet of time ... and the image of a spotted new fawn, at pillow height, next to my hospital bed.

* * *

For fifty-five years, I was told, and believed, it had been all my
fault.

"How old were you when it happened?" people would ask.

"A baby. One year, two months."

It might have been a good plan if dribs and drabs of the story hadn't leaked—my father's temper, the eight-cup percolator coffeepot thrown in rage at my mother but finding its mark on my chest and arms as I clung to her skirt—changing my life from that moment on. The truth about the "accident" came too late for me to do anything about it anyway.

You know what? I wish I didn't know. It bugs me that I can't confront him now. "I'm sorry, Annie," might have helped.

★ ★ ★

Dr. Buchanan, the Naval Hospital surgeon who treated me for years, told my parents that I would require multiple surgeries as I matured. My skin would become a tight fit as I grew.

Contracting scars, thick like rubber bands, made it almost impossible to throw a baseball or, sometimes, to take a deep breath. In theory, intermittent skin grafts and versatile "Z-Plasty" surgical techniques could lessen the constriction.

New York, 1954. I was twelve years old.

The operating table felt cold and hard, but it was the sickening anesthetic gas, ether, that I hated. I battled the oncoming blackness, needing to breathe but trying to postpone the inevitable last gasp, struggling to see through Vaseline-coated eyes into the looming shadows.

I strained to remain focused on the upside-down face hovering above me, trying to blink a signal that he was pressing down too hard on my nose—but I couldn't move. I wanted to continue listening to the muffled voice of the anesthesiologist telling me to "count down from ten," a trick I knew well—coaxing me to inhale the nauseating anesthetic as the black, acrid rubber mask enveloped my face.

Click-whoosh … click-whoosh … the sounds, my vision, and thoughts blurred into the darkness—the way they always did.

The children's ward in St. Albans General Hospital became my part-time home since that year I needed five surgeries. The ward was a beautiful place, a long rectangular room with huge windows that made the walls glow like a strawberry peach sunset. A sleek, white linoleum aisle separating boys from girls was shiny and smooth, making me wish for my clip-on roller skates. Each side of the ward had been partitioned into six four-bed, semi-private square cubicles, separated by half-walls to bed height and topped with another three feet of clear glass.

We kids were fascinated by local artists transforming the glass panels. They painted scenes of huge rabbits in colorful, big-buttoned jackets hiding Easter eggs in April; brilliant foliage in autumn; goblins and pumpkins for Halloween; Santa's reindeer with a bright red sleigh overflowing with Christmas toys; and spinning dreidel tops during Chanukah.

My favorite painting depicted a tiny, spotted fawn curled up, asleep on a patch of grass, right at pillow height on my glass partition in spring. I was fortunate enough to enjoy all four seasons of creative window art that year.

Surgical procedures never frightened me. But I learned to dread the authoritarian nurse who hid her anger behind an extra push on a syringe or the nurse's aide intolerant of a little girl who dared to complain, "It hurts too much, please stop!"

Ah, and then there was Miss Kuhn, a nurse reminiscent of Florence Nightingale, the founder of modern nursing. She was so very pretty, with the blackest hair, good humor, a special sort of kindness, and the sweetest cherry-lipped smile imaginable. We jockeyed for position when her rounds allowed her the extra time to administer the mandated three injections a day of antibiotics, not a small feat in the 1950s. She was the Pied Piper of our ward.

Non-disposable needles were thick and brittle and frequently broke in our arms in the less skilled hands of aides-in- training.

She was great with a needle—it hardly hurt. A swift, straight-on jab and bingo! Done. Nurse Kuhn became a savior of sorts. A gem of a person, skillful, with the bonus of caring for kids who had already experienced more troubles than most people do in a lifetime.

I was lucky enough to have a bed next to a large window with a deep sill where a plant could grow—prime real estate in the ward, a status symbol showing off my longevity in the hospital. The simple attrition of other kids and my willingness to deliver towels to the bedsides of the non-ambulatory kids didn't hurt either. Seniority benefits, I thought.

The small chores I was given and the way the kids admired me made me proud.

My window overlooked a roof a few floors below, which I imagined as a humongous pinball machine. The spinning air vents shaped like a queen's crown, pipes, and metal stacks served as flippers and bumpers. Long hours whizzed by when I became a heroine in my make-believe game, where, from behind the window, I didn't need my bandaged arms to play.

"Come down from there, Anna!" Nurse Kuhn broke into my imaginary world and walked toward me to scoot me down from my perch on the windowsill. "You're pressed too tight up against the glass; it's not meant for that."

"Okay, but … but, I don't get to see outside anymore. I'm here over a month," I whined as I slid from the cozy hideaway, pulling my pillow after me. "And … and"—my lip trembled—"mostly everybody else gets to go home. Why do I always have to stay here?" I started to sob quietly so as not to disturb anyone sleeping.

She leaned into the opening and studied the roof below. "Too bad there's only a roof you have to look at, huh?" She understood how lonesome I felt, especially since one of my best friends would be discharged the next morning. Billy's parents were taking him home after we'd been friends for six months. He could almost walk by himself now.

"What were you doing?"

"Playing Superhero-Pinball." I nodded toward the lower rooftop. "Look."

She rested her hands on the sill and leaned in. "Doesn't it remind you of a huge pinball game down there?" I asked. "I start the game with two heroes and let them use their superpowers to ricochet over the bumpers and flippers only I can activate through mental telepathy. It gets really exciting, Miss Kuhn!"

She chuckled. "Yes, I understand. So, who are you in the game?"

I felt good again. I bristled and crouched to pounce. "Look at me," I whispered in a rough theatrical voice. "Da-dah! The amazing Human Pinball, with superpowers beyond belief! BUZZZ ... ZAP ... BOING ... SPLAT!"

I mimicked the cartoon characters on TV as I shuffled around in my bunny slippers, pinging back and forth between my bed and the wall—caught up in the game of "let's pretend."

"Good heavens!" She clasped her hands together, cocked her head, looking like she was thinking of the possibilities. "And, who would I be in your game?"

"Obviously, Wonder Woman, the warrior princess of the Amazons!" We muffled our laughter as she spun around, just like Wonder Woman would have.

"And your Lasso of Truth is your stethoscope!" Everyone knew it was impossible to lie if you were caught in the golden lasso. "And ... let me think. Your cap is your tiara, another lethal weapon. And ... and, your indestructible bracelets are full of high-energy power, in a flash ready to fend off the enemy! But ... where's your invisible plane?"

"Ah-ha! I'll tell you where I keep it later." With a twinkle in her eye, she smiled and pointed skyward. "I want you to promise me something." The way she looked at me and tilted my face toward hers meant business.

"I know you. You're strong, a survivor. Don't give in to self- pity. Everyone gets scars, some on the inside, some on the outside. Your tomorrows belong only to you. Make them count.

"Promise me … you'll think about it?"

I puffed out my cheeks, exhaled. "Yup, I promise." I leaned into my window, studied the roof below, and thought about Nurse Kuhn, and Wonder Woman.

My home away from home proved energetic, loving and full of adventure. Although the trials of life revolving around hospitals seem daunting to some, I adapted. Those experiences taught me to look beyond words and first impressions, to empathize deeply, and stand with those who couldn't stand up for themselves.

Just like Wonder Woman.

★ ★ ★

Pounding rain and low, dark clouds hugged our ward in late October. I eagerly got back to the Nancy Drew mystery I'd recently borrowed from the lending library wagon. The volunteer candy striper was becoming my friend, and hot commodity mysteries featuring the girl sleuth usually arrived at my bed first. The latest, *The Secret at Shadow Ranch*, had horses, a ranch, and a dark secret; nothing could be more exciting.

My hand halted between the pages of the detective mystery. I thought about my mother's visit earlier that day and glanced fondly at the lifelike plaster-of-Paris horse she brought, now prancing next to my plant on the windowsill. The strain had been visible around her blue eyes, yet she never complained about the arduous two-bus trip to visit me three times a week.

"Look, I brought you a new ribbon." Her soft curls bounced as she laughed and flashed the satiny pink prize in front of me. "Feel it." She tempted me to reach for it.

I giggled back at her, knowing she wanted me to stretch the scars on my arms. I was no dummy!

Goosebumps followed each loving stroke of the hairbrush on my scalp. She filled me in on what my twin sister, Mary, was up to and how happy my fancy guppies were in their new fish tank. I started feeling lonely for my mom halfway through the visit when she packed my pajamas and laundry into a valise. She blew me one last kiss before leaving the ward.

Now, I reached slowly, carefully, for the new ribbon in my hair. Pleased, I continued to read.

Clunk! Something metal dropped and wobbled loudly to a stop. A bedpan, maybe? The unusual commotion made me jump.

"*Ouch!*" I yanked the tape that held foam compression bandages across my chest and arms and squinted to see through rows of glass walls toward the nurses' station at the far end of the ward. Medical personnel were rushing equipment to the rarely used critical care suite and the bedside of a new surgical patient.

Those of us who could get out of our beds gathered in the center aisle. The new girl from the next cubicle, Sandie, beat me there.

"What's going on?" I asked.

"It sounds terrible. Let's go see," Sandie said.

She sidled up to the wall, and I stooped to a stealth position so that I could follow her down the aisle. We sneaked toward the isolated area unobserved, where we were able to witness the unfolding tragedy in the off-limits area of the ward.

The boy's turban-like head bandage looked eerily lit from above, as was the upturned, tortured face of his father, begging for a do-over of this day. His arms moved in rhythm with the sobs of the boy's mother as he held her, trying to rub out her screaming grief. Their faces were so close, they blended. I wondered about how unusual it seemed to see grown-ups touching like that.

Suddenly, the double doors of the ward boomed open. The swoosh of a black, floor-length cassock kept time with the clack of rosary beads as a priest rushed past us into the room. I saw his panic and tension, but mostly the way his white-knuckled hand clutched a prayer book close to his chest. His body language told the story. He passed Sandie and me as if we didn't exist, contrary to what I remembered of his friendly nature.

The scene beyond the doorway darkened, the people becoming merely shadows.

The priest spoke softly to the couple as he bowed over the blanketed patient and spread his arms wide over the boy's body. His robe seemed to absorb any light left in the room as he prayed. The boy's parents continued to sob. The last drawn-out wail from the woman— "my Bobby"—hung in the air and wouldn't go away.

Abruptly, all turned quiet, as if the hands of God were raised for silence. It was over. Activity stopped—sounds hushed. People stayed in place, like a theatrical performance, while descending draperies shrouded the stage at the end of a play.

Our faces were tear-streaked as we held hands and continued to watch, too sad to talk.

★ ★ ★

Clergy of all denominations visited us on a routine basis. On the day the boy died, we overheard a remark by the priest to one of the nurses. The priest's eyes appeared red and strained. "He has not been baptized and will not have the rights to Heaven," he said, distressed.

"What? Can that be true?" I asked Sandie in a hushed voice. "How would I know? I wish we didn't hear it," she mumbled, annoyed.

We never got the chance to ask where exactly the priest thought the boy would go. Although my sister Mary and I attended Catholic school, the conversation bewildered me.

That night, I stared at the stars and found the outermost star in the handle of the Little Dipper: Polaris, the North Star. I studied the sky and thought of the tragic events of the day and the puzzling remark about baptism. I mulled over the lessons I had learned in parochial school and knew that questioning doubts showed a serious lack of faith, punishable by something.

But, as usual, I couldn't help it. I was growing tired of saying, "I'm sorry."

Sure, Sister Nicodemus taught us in third grade that more than "three bad thoughts" a day would land me in Purgatory— if I got lucky. A correctional spiritual halfway house of sorts, I suppose. Worse yet, Hell was the dreaded destination for greater infractions and disobedience, where "You'll really find out what it feels like to be burned!"

I'm not sure what frightened me more, the idea of another go-round with painful burns or the insensitive nun's arthritic finger snaking close to my nose like a wizard's wand full of destructive powers.

The ward was quiet and, oh, so sad. It took a few days before some of the kids gathered in my glass-enclosed cubicle. A few of the kids questioned if God would send the young brain-injured boy someplace other than Heaven for not being baptized. We needed to talk about it. Two wheelchairs and a stick-out shoulder cast made it a tight fit. We concluded God wouldn't abandon the boy. The priest couldn't be right.

"Maybe we heard wrong?" Sandie said.

Norman said, "Have you ever thought about he might be Jewish, huh? Jews don't get baptized. I don't understand all the fuss." Nevertheless, the idea of a place like Hell worried him.

We questioned everything in hushed voices and decided to ask for Nurse Kuhn's opinion.

She sat at the edge of my bed; the faint crackling sound of her heavily starched uniform comforted me. She realized most of us were familiar with death, even taking bets on which one of us would be next. But the boy had died too suddenly, and we weren't prepared.

"What do you think, Nurse Kuhn? Is the boy in Hell now?" little Viola asked shyly.

The small girl hardly smiled, so it was surprising when she spoke up. My heart had ached when it was rumored her parents gave her up for adoption. We didn't know much about her accident, only that she tripped into a bucket of roofer's hot tar. Now seven, she had been in the ward longer than anyone. It was sad that she never had visitors.

It must have hurt when she cried, or tried to laugh. Even when I weaved her frizzy hair into ribbon-laced braids away from the damaged side of her face, she mostly snuffled. I wanted to hold and protect her and often wondered at the nature of some people who, simply by not caring, were cruel.

Norman made one of his I'm-disgusted-at-how-stupid-this-is looks, and cut in. "Just because the priest said it, doesn't make it true," he blurted, maneuvering his twisted leg for comfort.

Nurse Kuhn was serious, pausing to look at each of us, aware of the profound implications her answer would have. Surprisingly, her face lit up with a little smile. "I don't believe he went to Hell at all. Bobby's free now, in no pain, most likely making friends in a beautiful place, maybe like Heaven. Now, let's talk about your feelings." She redirected the chat session into a therapeutic conversation until the squeaky rubber wheels of the food cart signaled dinnertime.

Close to four o'clock in the morning, before early shifts changed players, silence finally cloaked our beds. I prayed for some answers to the whys in life.

My rare one-on-one with God felt good, so I decided to push my position a bit and ask for intervention for Mary and Mom. "I'm okay here, but what about Mary? She just sits at home and doesn't say anything while Dad yells at them. And then he wants her to sit on his lap. I don't understand what's going on. He's always so angry at us and ridicules Mom for just about everything.

"It's not fun to be home anymore. And, um … it scares me when he gets the strap out. He broke two of my wire stitches last time. The truth is, God, I'm starting to jump every time his hands go for his belt buckle." In my father's hands, a simple pants belt could become a weapon. "I don't understand why this and why that," I chattered on, gesturing for effect. Then, I coyly slipped in the big request. "Oh, by the way, uh, would it be possible to jam the buckle on his belt?"

Oops! It dawned on me I topped the "three bad thoughts" limit that day. But just maybe, since God liked me quite a lot and I finally turned to Him for help, I could gain some wiggle room.

I talked and talked. Hot tears pooled down my cheeks, thinking of my twin at home, alone without me. I held tight to Boopkins, the doll Mom brought me from Mary. I missed my sister every hour of every day. But fear of infection kept kids, even family, from visiting the wards. Excellent for disease prevention, but terrible for the lonely souls inside.

I chatted on and on to someone I absolutely knew in my heart was paying attention, probably sitting on a cloud or something, watchful and relaxed. I asked for suggestions to make my next home visit a warm, loving time. Truth was, I felt guilty for wanting to stay in the hospital with my friends and wished Mary could be part of it.

I can't remember when I became aware of Nurse Kuhn standing at the foot of my bed. She heard me talk to God in the bright blue light of the full moon. Shy and embarrassed at being found out, our eyes connected. Sensing my dilemma, she nodded, backed into the shadows, and disappeared.

She was a perfect bit of Heaven on gum-soled shoes.

Chapter 4

"I Promise ..."

I couldn't be certain if our pup, Kaya, fussed over the newcomer as a matter of instinct or because she wanted a four-legged friend of her own. Padding in and out of the shower cubicle, she sniffled, licked, and finally cuddled down against the fawn's chest to wait.

We kept a goat milk formula on hand for the alpaca babies needing a nutritional boost. Goat milk was easier to digest than cow's milk. As usual, I added a spoonful of honey to the warm mixture and filled the cleverly designed reservoir-type bottle nipple that squeezed nourishment into any baby incapable or too weak to suckle.

Her head wobbled in my hand as my fingers traced a pattern from the white snippet of hair just above her nose, up the natural groove between her eyes, around each ear, and down her neck. The fawn innocently gazed up at me, then at little Kaya—with no sign of fear.

Poor baby. The tug on my heart was real, an ache for her and for the mother she would never know.

"You're safe now," I murmured. "I'll take good care of you. I promise."

Did I imagine the faint scent of a baby?

"What if I call you Huckleberry? Hmm ..."

I jiggled the bottle's nipple into the side of her mouth and squeezed a bit of milk on her tongue. She swallowed, then coughed. I held, patted, and soothed her like I would a human baby with congested lungs. *Can a deer suffer from asthma?* I hoped she inherited some of the crucial immunity her mother's colostrum would have provided within the first twenty-four hours of her life.

"Sorry, I have to examine you." I slid my pinky finger between her jaws and probed for a cleft palate deformity in the bony roof of her mouth. Normal.

It was a clear, sunny afternoon. I bundled the fawn in my arms and brushed my lips against the top of her head, whispering calmly, "Sunshine is good for you." She wiggled her leg over my forearm and pressed her neck against mine. The outside door opened directly into the kitchen. I carried her and passed Caruso, quiet on his perch for a change.

"Hi, my bird."

He was a happy parrot. "Wanna go to the opera?" Caruso's green and yellow head feathers fluffed, he flapped his wings, stared at the fawn, and scuttled down toward the door latch of his cage. He wanted out.

"Nope, not now." In good weather, we let him loose along the top of the wood security fence around our pool, where he strutted through a tangle of wisteria vines singing Christmas songs or yodeling a tune from one of the "learn how to" tapes I bought, for me. Although Pino kept his flight-feathers clipped, Caruso sometimes managed to fly into downhill trees, where he paced along the branches, screaming for help. We left a ladder and a jump-on-to-stick handy because Caruso didn't like heights.

One slow step at a time, I crossed the narrow deck and descended to our isolated fenced-in garden, where the grass was lush because our horses couldn't get to it. I eased the fawn down in a shady area beneath a large yellow poplar tree. She watched alert, fascinated by the long-bearded iris blooms backlit by the sun. Her large ears tracked the sounds of her world: the chirp of a robin, the rustle of leaves, the scream from Caruso to "let me outta here," and Kaya sniffling at her face.

Although I helped her stand by hugging her to me, within seconds her body was racked by another coughing episode, and she collapsed. Weak, exhausted, but breathing, she rested. Seeing her in such distress broke my heart, but fifteen minutes later, I helped her try again. "Front first, rear end next, and ... up you come. Good girl, I've got you." With one hand supporting her ribcage, I rhythmically thumped her sides. I could hear the blockage in her lungs breaking up. From a raspy crackle to a less definitive crunch, as one would hear as a hardboiled egg was peeled.

She shuddered on her splayed-out forelegs and leaned forward slightly until, with one final croup-like *craaack*, the mucus released its hold on her airway. She dropped to her knees and fell the rest of the way to the grass, took her first deep breath, and closed her eyes to sleep.

"*Aehh ...*" She hiccupped.

"How's she doing?" Pino hurried down the steps toward us, waving the baby milk bottle. "I warmed it." His smile went from ear to ear.

"Her lungs cleared—poor little thing. There's something else, though. Look at the size of her gut! Last night it was flat!"

He bent to stroke her side and touched the edges of her belly. "I see a pot belly," he teased. He turned to me. "Won't more milk make it worse?"

"Food takes priority. The next problem will be getting her to empty that bladder." I remembered thirteen days of traumatizing catheterization when my gastrointestinal functions stalled after one stressful surgery. The frantic actions of the medical staff made it clear the situation was potentially catastrophic.

"Pino, remember my nickname from Fire Rescue? I was thinking of naming her Huckleberry."

"You name everything Huckleberry." He gave me a quizzical look and handed me the plastic bottle. "Doesn't work for me."

I slid the nipple between her lips and squeezed a bit of warm milk on her tongue. "C'mon, this is healthy stuff." Startled, she focused her full attention on the new sensation.

Her body rippled into motion—ears pricked forward, eyes wide and focused—followed by a soft, begging, "*Aehh ... aehh.*" Her tongue instinctively took on a life of its own, curling up on the sides like a spoon. It flipped around, probing for more.

"How about you!" I giggled when she shifted to a front kneel, butt-up position. Another squeeze on the nipple was followed by one more swallow, then another and another. One empty bottle later, I mimicked the baseball announcer I remembered in Fenway Park. "Folks, the bases are loaded, and this baby's coming home!

"Hey, guess what! I just thought of how we can help her to pee. I should have thought about it before. All I have to do is copy what our alpaca mothers do with their babies!"

"But, they lick their rear ends!" Pino cocked his head in contemplation and shot me a comical look. "Uh-oh!"

I licked my lips and smirked.

"You're not!" He laughed, an infectious laugh, chuckling at first, then spilling over into a rollicking free-for-all.

The soft grass on the fawn's body made the fawn squiggle with her head lifted toward the warmth of the sun's rays. She stood, hesitated, and wobbled toward us, tail pointed up. Her legs bowed out radically in the rear. I suspected her gut muscles were cramping.

"Does your belly hurt?"

"*Aehh* ..." the fawn said, expecting us to know what her discomfort was all about.

Ah, but we did know.

I kissed her nose and stroked her bony rear end, as her mother would have, from her bottom to the tip of her straight-up white tail, over and over.

"*Aehh* ..." She gazed at me quizzically and started to get what I asked her to do. She maneuvered her rear end slowly, swaying into a steady rocking motion, shivering from the strain, and spread her legs.

Nothing happened.

"Aw, baby," I murmured, running my hands over her body. A soothing song my mother taught me in the hospital came to mind.

After one surgery, an inexperienced nurse's aide suspended my arm to a horizontal pole above my bed by a single binding gauze wristlet. I was in agony.

"Mama, my hand!" I cried when I saw my mother through a blur of tears.

She called for help and tried to release the cutting noose from my wrist, using her shoulder and arm as leverage under my shoulders to release the pressure. I breathed her wild rose fragrance when she lay her head on my pillow next to mine, her chin quivering as she whispered the song I now softly sang to the tiny fawn.

"'A' You're Adorable, and ..."

By the time I got to "F, you're a feather in my arms," it finally happened.

A welcome stream of warm urine flowed—and flowed—while she stood motionless, spent from the effort. She sighed and uttered a long "*ahh*..." which, this time, meant relief.

Delighted at her accomplishment, she jumped a little, scrunching her eyes tight when Kaya's tongue homed in for a second go 'round on her face.

Kaya lay down in front of her, nose to nose.

"Hang in there, girly," I said. The response was sweet. The baby kneeled, lifted her butt unsteadily, back legs bowed out, and she wobbled up. Lowering her head toward the tiny dog, she kissed Kaya right back.

That's when her passion for kissing started. I'm sure of it.

The fawn adapted quickly to her surroundings. We had anticipated panic, waking up in a confined area without her mother. It never showed up. She had known her mother's love for scarcely a few hours, yet she accepted affection without fear or reservation from us.

"Will you look at them?" Pino said for the umpteenth time. "They're not only grooming—they're bonding."

Later, we watched the dog and the deer discover the iris garden together, their faces appearing, then disappearing as they wandered about, poking in and out of the tall green plants. The fawn stretched to inspect the flower heads but could not reach them. She appeared like a flower blossom herself.

Her name just popped into my mind. "How about calling her Blossom?"

"That's perfect!"

The best names just take time.

★ ★ ★

The sunset was brilliant that evening. Pino settled comfortably into a club chair in front of the den windows and held his wine glass to the light. "One heck of a day."

The wine tasted peachy, just like it looked. I sat cross-legged on the carpet, wholly engrossed in the how-to booklet of the new video camera Mary gave me.

"Watch out!" Pino grabbed my wine glass just as Blossom reached me.

Her wet nose trailed around my face, and she licked my ears. It tickled. She kept nuzzling and pushing on my lap until her long front legs settled on my shoulders. *"Aehh ..."* and her very wet nose planted on my cheek!

"Hey, was that a kiss? Is this the way you say, 'Let's be friends?'" I sealed the precious moment in my memory.

I heard her breath and felt her chest push against mine. As my hands gentled her body, I allowed myself to revel in the sheer bliss of it all. She pulled away and, not four inches from my face, gazed steadily into my eyes. In wonderment, I could feel her trust and her instinctual yearning to bond and interact.

Compassion filled me, and I knew a bridge had been crossed—a shift that would form the basis for change in both of our lives—as I held the not-so-wild animal in my arms.

Tiny Footprints

There are footprints, tiny footprints across my heart.
I'm not sure how they arrived. I should remember
being trod upon, like a rug or path. I should know
who came my way marking me with their passing.

There are small clues, a certain tenderness
when I am with you; a certain love of all
that is hidden from the eye and felt
with the soul. Have you been running
through my sand, a playful child, barefoot, and

joyful with the grit of me between your toes?
Have you made tunnels and castles, burying your-self
neck-deep in my life? I have to ask. You see,
there are footprints, tiny footprints across my heart
and I'm not sure how they arrived.

— Jeanne Hamilton Troast

Chapter 5

Here Comes Blossom!

Don't ask me why—I don't have the words. Why does someone begin to respond to a baby that yearns to be loved?

By the time the first glimmer of sun, songbird chatter, and the mellow *coo-OO-oo* of mourning doves started howdy-doin' each other, the pattering of fawn feet had closed in, and a breathy, wet nose nudged my pillow.

No use pretending to be asleep. I opened one eye to peek at Blossom's curious gaze, wicked with puppy playfulness, reminding myself she was real, and a deer. I held back and stayed the urge to tickle her. Instead, I *boink … boink'd* my finger off her nose. There was no suggestion of body odor. Nothing like the "horsey" scent that clung to my clothing when I put my arms around my horse's neck.

"Good morning, Blossom," I said and yawned. As usual, she yawned back at me. Her eyes fixed on mine, teasing, waiting me out. She didn't move. Neither did I. And, then the inevitable licking and wet-nosed snuffling started. I rolled away from her compulsive grooming habits. She followed on a mission to get the job done right.

Pino came into the bedroom holding two cups of coffee. "I figured she'd get you going."

"How long have you been up?"

"About as long she's been resting there on your pillow."

I wiped my face and scooched back to lean against the headboard.

"I thought it was you!" I joked and stuck my tongue out at him.

At four months, Blossom weighed close to forty pounds and drank over two quarts of milk a day, chomped for the most part on grass and horse chow, and had a passion for raw vegetables, nuts, fruits, the crunch of salted chips, and cold cereal, mostly Cheerios.

Her young body grew strong and muscled, with polka-dotted fur transitioning into a sleek tawny coat, begging to be stroked.

An atmosphere of excitement—a sense of adventure—filled the house.

Breakfast had become a smorgasbord of healthy granolas and fruits, sometimes shared on the front steps of the house before joggers, bikers, and other morning exercise enthusiasts took to the single-lane rural streets of Tewksbury.

"She's a refined, laid-back personality type, don't you think?" I asked Pino one morning.

"Huh?" Blossom communicated through eye contact, a soft bump from her nose, body, or a series of sounds and actions that left no doubt as to what she wanted. And, she wanted his cereal.

"*Aehh* ..." she begged.

"Okay, but don't dump it." He held a paper napkin under her chin, ready to catch the splatter. Instead, she opened her mouth and gently pulled the food off the spoon with her upper lip.

"Not even a slurp!" I said. "She's learning, by copying? Do it again."

"There goes my breakfast. Her stomach is a bottomless pit." Runners were out early one bright morning. Our neighbor,

Nancy, was included in the bunch, jogging around the corner. She waved.

"Whatcha doing?" she called in a cheerful voice and detoured over the lawn. "Good morning." She leaned to tousle Blossom's head, then kissed her on the nose. "Lots of people talking about you, little one." She looked up at us. "So, now she eats from a spoon?"

We spoke about town politics, the upcoming hunting season, and our plans for Blossom. She seemed at a loss for words at the predicament we faced. "I thought you were going to keep her a secret, and in the house?"

"Can't do that to a wild animal—" Pino began.

"In or out, as long as she wants to stay," I interrupted, lowering my gaze from Blossom's eyes to her wagging tail. She liked Nancy. "We walk and explore the woods every day with her, so she gets a sense of her surroundings. We're not holding her back. If she decides to leave, we won't—couldn't—stop her anyway. Nope, it has to be up to her."

"Sometimes, our feelings get in the way," Pino tried to lighten the mood. He put his arm around my shoulders to show solidarity, I suppose.

Worry creased Nancy's forehead. "We don't know how you're going to protect her. Jaime and I will spread the word. We've been here a long time and know many of the hunters in the area, but I can't promise they'll be friendly to the idea. Besides, in season, hunters come from out of state. Jaime thinks there are a few with big enough egos who—" The grim expression on my face stopped her. "Sorry."

"We know."

As the days and weeks passed, a network of people we probably never would have met, walked, jogged, or waved as they drove by, trying to get a glimpse of the friendly little fawn from Tewksbury.

A rumble, like a load of melons rolling down the stairs, signaled Blossom's latest attempt to navigate the staircase to our office.

"Ba da boom, ba da bing," Pino said, opening his arms, waiting for her to poke her head around the corner and into his arms. "Here comes Blossom." He scratched her neck and opened the door to the garden.

I was about to sit down and get back to my work when he signaled me over. "Blossom's got company."

"The old doe again?"

Nodding, he said, "Just like the day before, and the day before that. "Wonder if they're related."

"Aehh..." Blossom called to the doe and scampered off without hesitation.

We named the doe Claire. White hair circled her dark, bulging eyes. I wondered how she survived long enough to grow old in a hunting area like Tewksbury, where deer lived an average life of about one and a half years. Maybe being a not-so-pretty collectible was a good thing sometimes?

Blossom's tail remained straight up and fluttering while she licked Claire's mouth. The same submissive behavior is common in young horses. In turn, the doe groomed and nuzzled her with the tenderness of a mother, at times holding her steady with one front leg, continuing to do-si-do around until she was satisfied that the fawn was groomed up correctly.

Claire jerked to attention when we came out of the office, but after a moment, a peaceful aura of acceptance seemed to soften her body, and she resumed nuzzling her little friend.

"Go slow." I led the way to a shady area where Pino had hung a hammock between two massive poplars. With my legs dangling and feet touching the ground, we rocked into a slow, steady swing. A bewildering sadness crept over the idyllic scene as I contemplated that Blossom might leave with the doe, guided by instinct to be with her own kind, and not return.

"Don't worry." Pino squeezed my hand. "She loves us."

Claire stayed an hour or more, meandering down the hill with Blossom, into the trees behind the barn. Blossom hesitated for an instant at the wood line, spun, tail high, and scampered back to us.

The following day, Claire brought twin fawns with her. I was rolling apples for Blossom to chase when they showed up—no doubt about it. The deer were coming closer to observe us—as we discovered them. They stood like statues, guarded, heads high, while their noses sniffed for trouble. Little feet stomped in agitation, and white bushy tails flicked, anticipating a quick getaway. They were perplexed when Blossom socialized back and forth between us, as if she were trying to bridge existing natural boundaries.

I tried to soothe them. "*Ooo* ... you kids are so tough! Pretty babies."

They sniffed Blossom and waited for a signal to flee from Claire. When that didn't happen, they relaxed and started to enjoy the apples. I saw no aggressive behavior, only three little bobbing heads, like those silly plastic birds I remembered, mechanically dipping their heads up-down, up-down, in and out of a glass of water.

Blossom had outgrown the bed she shared with Kaya and now slept on a large padded mat in the kitchen. Satisfied that she would not wreck the house, the "doggie" gates came down.

"You have to see what's going on with the troops." Pino chuckled, bent low in an exaggerated crouch. "Follow me."

"You look like a knuckle dragger." I poked him and stooped to mimic his chimp-like actions. Ambient light muted the bright yellow wallpaper as we tiptoed barefoot past the open dining area into the kitchen.

"Aw." I held a finger to my lips. One toy-sized dog and one forty-pound fawn cuddled within the confines of Kaya's cushy doggie bed caught some Z's. Blossom's body filled most of the space; everything else—head, legs. and backside—hung over the sides. As tight as a puzzle piece, Kaya's bottom was tucked close to Blossom's belly, her head resting on the fawn's side, one ear up. She was snoring in tempo with Blossom's breathing. I gestured to Pino that I was going for the video camera.

"Snooper," Pino chided when I returned with my camera and a utility belt with extra batteries and cassettes.

The familiar tap of deer footsteps on the kitchen tiles was a sure sign my photo op was history. "How did Caruso get out of his cage?" Blossom and Kaya were scrambling to avoid our yellow-naped Amazon parrot, who was waddling in a two-step toward them, wings spread wide, trying to nip at their feet. "Darn it, Caruso," I said. He stopped when he saw me.

Spreading his multi-colored tail feathers, he stood as tall as he could on three-inch legs and stretched his neck. "Wanna go to the opera?"

"Okay, Caruso, let me hear you go to the opera." I went through the routine he expected. He strutted in circles as he performed his repertoire of songs.

Caruso was a blast. "Blaa-fum, Kaya! Peeno, Aaannnaaa ... Oh, the opera! Woopy tawdry ... woopy tawdry." He trilled his voice in an impressive vibrato, trying to mimic the sounds of my favorite operatic music of Italy.

"Can you talk like a rooster? Cock-a-doodle-doooooo." Caruso was on a roll. "Ol' McDonald had a farm ... Ee-I-ee-I-oooo—with a quack, quack here an' a quack, quack there ... I'm dreaming of a white Christmas ..."

This place is like a zoo!

"Okay, Caruso, time to go back to your house." Pino urged the parrot on his fingers, swooped him over his head, and then let him step to his perch next to the kitchen window.

"Can you yodel?" Caruso mimicked before dipping deep into his seed dish, content with the ruckus he'd created.

"Come on, girls, who's going outside?"

Blossom languidly crossed the gravel driveway to the grass while Kaya made a beeline to her favorite spot near the dogwood tree. The little dog made life in our home a lot easier by showing Blossom, by example, how to wait by the door when she needed to "go."

As afternoon turned into evening, the picture on the Lemon Fantasy bubble bath bottle promised a relaxing spa-like atmosphere. The bathtub was built into an alcove, with a picture window facing a tiny secluded garden where Blossom sometimes napped, curled up on the pachysandra ground cover. She wasn't there.

I lit a row of candles on the glass shelf next to the windowsill and turned on a meditation tape. Total relaxation had become an indulgence. I allowed my thoughts to drift within the mellow, spiritual tones of wooden flutes, my body soaking under a thick layer of scented lemon meringue suds.

A snort and a splash of suds put an end to my tranquility. Who knew Blossom liked bubbles?

Chapter 6

First Threat

I was at my desk when some kind of scratching sound coming from the office door made my blood go cold.

I glanced up and yelped.

The man's face was distorted, flattened tight against the door screen. Bright noonday sun backlit his bulky shape, turning a mop of blond hair into a ghoulish halo. Barely distinguishable eyes peered through the screen at me.

I rolled my eyes and groaned when I recognized him.

Eddy continued to scrape at the screen, with long, slow pulls from his fingernails, as if it pleased him. I heard him laugh.

Why didn't he just knock?

"Eddy, stop that!" Annoyed at the interruption, I pushed away from my computer, got up quickly.

"Hey. Pino called yesterday about closing the pool for the winter. Told him I'd come by today."

"Wait a moment," I said. Too late.

Eddy jiggled the door handle and walked in, allowing the door to slam behind him.

What nerve. I backed away.

"Got to get the pool cover out of storage." He nodded toward the unfinished basement area, grinned with a disquieting in-your-face intensity, took a step closer, and extended his hand.

I remembered Eddy's Plumbing and Pool and his company's slogan: "Your Water is our Bread and Butter." Eddy was fortyish, a hardworking, rugged outdoorsman-type with an easy smile, and at times, went out of his way to be funny. To me, he acted hot-wired and downright annoying.

"Sorry if I startled you. Forgive me?"

"Not a chance," I said. "Hi." I shook his hand and glanced at the image of a twelve-point buck silkscreened on his tee shirt and the green and brown camo pants he wore.

Eddy walked around the small office, looked at books stacked on pine shelves, at the brick fireplace hearth crammed with files, and at Pino's leather-topped desk, a fond remnant of his past corporate life. He leaned over, tracing his fingers thoughtfully across the wood carving scrollwork on one corner. "Very nice."

He pulled a notepad and pen to the edge of the desk, scribbled something, ripped it from the pad, and shook it for me to take. "Here's my number if you need to reach me. I'm out of cards."

"Sure, Eddy, help yourself." I managed to grin at his arrogance and nodded at his tee shirt.

"Going hunting?"

"Yup. Pretty soon. As a matter of fact, I want permission to hunt your property."

"Nope, sorry. We don't allow—"

"Just asking." He appeared deflated. "Keeps the deer tick population down. Lyme disease an' all—"

"Truth is, I'm afraid of people hunting so close to our home. This farm is small, six plus acres, with alpacas and horses all over the place. And, just a week ago, our farrier luckily happened to duck down to shape a horseshoe and *zing!* Two bullet holes in his truck, right above where his head had been."

"You're kidding!" He shook his head. "Terrible. Always some crazy nut job out there. Me? I aim low—and I don't miss.

Never have to track a wounded deer to finish the job. Military training, and—"

"Never?" *Baloney.* My mind drifted. An uneasy silence followed. I picked up my sunglasses and headed for the door. "If only arrows and bullets had brains and could figure out where not to go, who not to kill, and how to pull the brake at the property line."

I told Eddy about an injured doe near our stream. "When she saw me, she panicked and struggled to stand on three legs, dragging her injured hind leg. An arrow was lodged in her rear hock joint. She limped away in pain and fear, and I never saw her again."

I noticed a playful, wide-eyed smugness in his expression. "And, speaking of hunting. You have a fawn in your yard behind the pool pump."

I froze. He had seen Blossom! Did he want to hunt *her*?

I was at a loss for words, then uttered impulsively, "She's

Blossom. She's been part of our family ever since ..." I held back. The only thing that made any sense was to try to arouse compassion in him—to let him see for himself. I had no good choices.

I forced myself to ask, "Would you like to meet her?"

"She'll come to you?" He followed me outside, enthusiastic and all smiles again.

"Blossom." My voice cracked.

Please don't answer.

"*Aehh...*" Blossom paused briefly before her high-stepping prance carried her down the stone stairway into the garden. Even a prima ballerina would envy her graceful athleticism.

"I'll be damned." Eddy stared and stooped in welcome when she approached us.

She's like a butterfly circling perilously close to the spider's web.

"You're sure a pretty little thing." He winked at her, enjoying the moment. He curled his fingers in a wave-like motion, massaging her chin, coaxing her face up toward his. Instead of turning away, she blinked at him and maintained eye contact.

Maybe I misjudged him.

"She likes me," he crooned. Blossom, who knew nothing but love and kindness from humans, responded by licking his hand.

A child can be taught not to take candy from a creepy guy. But a deer?

Blossom stood quietly, transfixed, watching Eddy as he tilted his head to the side and steadied her sweet face in one hand. Slowly and deliberately, he raised and cocked an imaginary gun and pointed it close to her head—between her eyes.

In horror, my ultimate fear for Blossom's life became a dress rehearsal for reality. I held my breath.

"*POW!*" He exhaled the word as the simulated recoil action of the phantom weapon jerked his arm in an upward arc.

"*Aeeehh ...*" Blossom shrieked, pulled back, whirled, fell, rolled, and crawled in a panicky effort to escape.

Eddy stepped back, laughing, as Blossom regained her footing and streaked down the hill toward the barn, white tail up, flagging her panic.

Blood pounded in my ears. Unable to hide my contempt, I reflexively struck out at him in anger and frustration.

"HOW DARE YOU!"

Eddy staggered back in surprise. His face splotched up with red patches, and suddenly, he became overly interested in his sneakers.

Never had I struck anyone in rage, and I was ashamed—almost, sort of. I whirled to face him. "What were you thinking?" I glared at him. "What's the matter with you?"

"I didn't mean to upset you." He apologized. "I was only joking. Sorry."

"Stow your apology," I shot back.

He was flustered, took a deep breath.

Another surge of frustration wouldn't let go. "You think this is a joke?" I demanded. "Know what? You scare me—not so much for me, but for her. Don't you know what you're doing? She's part of our family. We love her." I pleaded out the words and kicked at the grass in disgust. "So, tell me what I do now to protect her from someone who will pull the trigger without so much as a thought about the beautiful life they're blowing away?"

He lifted his hand in defense. "Wait, wait. Yeah, I understand."

I flinched when he put his hand on my arm. "I'm frightened because she's going to get shot, and I can't stop it!"

"But the truth is, you can do nothing. She's a deer and whether you like it or not, that's how it is."

"I can't stand the injustice," I said.

The anger churning in my gut surprised me. I looked away and squinted toward the far paddock where Justinian, Simba, and Protto Call were rearing and chasing each other in their own kind of horseplay. Blossom started to amble back up the hill toward us. I turned to Eddy.

"Please, look at her and tell me ... could you intentionally hurt her? I mean, you acted like you intended to kill her." I forced myself to look at him, pleading with my eyes. I needed to understand his motivation. For Blossom's sake, I forced myself to continue.

"No, of course not. It would be like shooting my dog Daisy. Besides, I would never shoot a fawn, or a doe with a fawn at its side," he said as if talking to himself. "I never thought about a deer having a personality. I never thought about a deer as a some-*one*—only as a some-*thing*."

He looked apologetic and asked, "You okay?"

I scowled at him. "Do I look like I'm okay?" I needed time.

Blossom returned to the house and grazed a few feet from us. "Eddy, see how she trusts you? Not being afraid of people could get her killed. When I see her, I see innocence, trust, and love. What do you see?" I asked.

"Always been an animal lover; you can ask anybody. Much rather take a picture to show my kid." Eddy shifted from one foot to the other. "So, have you also given thought to the other side of the population that likes the idea of deer in the community but worries there are too many of them eating their gardens?"

"And there are too many weapons in too many hands," I snapped.

"They're the same people who allow hunters on their property to save their landscaping."

We were at it again.

"There are lots of people you haven't met," I said. Those people who fear the sounds of gunfire and the implied threat—the people whose Sunday walks are splotched with don't-shoot-me orange vests."

Eddy cleared his throat. "Listen, I'm a careful hunter. I obey all laws. When I was a boy, I shot small game and squirrels."

I needed a breather and was glad for the change in tone. "You eat squirrel too, what, for a snack?" He didn't share my attempt at a bit of humor and gave me a wry look, then concentrated on Blossom, who was trying her utmost to untie his shoelace.

"Yes, we ate the squirrel," he continued dryly. "Are you a vegetarian?" Eddy regarded me for a long moment. "Because, if not, what makes you any different from any hunter? I hide in a tree stand to take a shot as casually as you walk down the meat aisle, looking for tenderloin. The result is the same."

He caught me off guard.

"You're kidding? I agree you have an argument, and I'm not a vegetarian. So, are you saying that everyone hunts basically because they're hungry or have a taste for what they kill? Hey, that's stock answer #1 in the book of 'If Anyone Asks Why You Hunt, Here's What You Say.'

"Think about it, Eddy. When was the last time you saw someone in a high-five frenzy at the butcher counter? And, come to think of it, no one's ever set up a photo shoot of me holding my freshly wrapped tenderloin ... suitable for framing!"

He glanced at his watch. "Got to get to work." A tight smile crossed his face. "My wife doesn't like to eat venison. The truth is I hunt because we have a great group of guys in our hunting club. Our group donates deer meat to feed the homeless, although I'll admit that many people don't much care for the flavor. You either do or you don't, I guess."

I was genuinely interested in where this conversation was going. "I saw your face when you faked shooting Blossom. Did you honestly think about eating her when you did that?" The tug on his shoelaces drew his attention back to his feet.

Blossom liked him.

Go figure.

"But," I said, "to think Blossom could be killed for nothing more than a sport, a bet, or a joke is intolerable to me. Her life means nothing to you, but to me, she means family. Because I can love a deer, I can be prosecuted, or worse, not even listened to? Does that make me weird to you?"

He spread his arms and let them slap to his sides. "But now, you and Blossom, well—it's different."

"Why is that?" I said. "Because I know her life should not end in a burp of satisfaction?"

His tone was tinged with sarcasm. "Only her? Why not save all the animals and promote world peace—like Miss America?"

"Simple. I wouldn't have a chance of making a difference with the powerful gun lobby group in the government. I'm only asking you to consider who she is before you pull the trigger."

He knelt to scratch her back. She stretched and wagged her tail in delight. "Hey, she wags her tail, just like Daisy."

The frown deepened the crease between his eyes. What he said next was thought-provoking, honest, and scared me to death.

"You know there's no way you can win this battle, so you'll have to come to terms with the fact that most people hunt for pleasure ... and to drag home the meat."

"Drag home the meat?" I was surprised at the words. "Do you really mean drag, as in prehistoric man drag?" I felt uneasy at the mental image of a Neanderthal man dragging an antelope back to his cave.

"Why not? Maybe." He shrugged. "My wife asks me all the time, too. She's a Bambi lover, just like you, so I've been thinking about it." He smiled. "This past season, I couldn't look into the eyes of the buck I shot. Mushed up over it. Must be gettin' old."

He remained quiet and thoughtful for a while and continued to scratch Blossom's back.

"Eddy? It looks like you could be a Bambi lover yourself."

"Maybe I am," he whispered to Blossom and flicked her ears.

★ ★ ★

Later, after barn check, Pino and I sat around a small wrought iron garden table and talked about the day.

Caruso was a puff of green and yellow as he strutted along the top of the six-foot fence surrounding the pool area. His favorite song, "I'm Dreaming of a White Christmas," usually made us laugh, but not this time. I was still off-balance from the day's events and continually made myself miserable by replaying the mock killing scene over and over.

"Now what, Blossom?" Pino said. The fawn maneuvered her head under Pino's hand and rested her face against his knee. Her large, violet-brown eyes projected contentment.

No longer could we pretend the threat to her life was not real, or that the time for action was infinite. I remembered Eddy's words when I asked if he could kill Blossom. Over and over, I replayed his words. "No, of course not, she's special. It would be like shooting my dog Daisy."

Blossom now had another admirer—hopefully, another protector. That realization was something I could hold on to. It was becoming clear Blossom was her own best advocate for survival—if we could keep her alive.

I thought about the guys down at the Oldwick General Store, schmoozing about the trophy deer and the promise of a good hunting season in the fields in Tewksbury.

Was this gentle fawn born merely to fuel the demand for another living target?

I felt sick.

Chapter 7

Not Just Any Deer

Deer are a shy, skittish species, and herd bound, or so I thought. Surprise! Blossom, our particular young deer, had an extraordinary personality: curious, interactive, playful, and she liked people.

A lot.

As word spread about the friendly doe who wagged her tail in greeting, we noticed a definite uptick in the walk, jog, and bike stats around Unicorn Hollow. Our corner of Fox Hill Road became a hub of activity on weekends when neighbors who worked in the towering buildings in and around New York City escaped into the hills of Tewksbury.

We were well aware that the downside of her generous personality and lack of fear was precisely what made her most vulnerable. But how were we supposed to protect her or keep her presence a secret while she created a local meet-and-greet welcoming committee with anyone who came to our farm?

After spending her first year and a half within the safe boundaries of our property, Blossom started to roam farther and for longer periods of time. In October, during the annual deer rut, her strong instincts kicked in.

I knew it was a Wednesday because, once again, the garbage truck created a racket when it backed into our new two-wheel trash bin. A few deer, including Blossom and Claire, scrambled up and over the ridge from the scene, zig-zagging beyond the back of the granite boulders. She didn't come home that evening, the next day, or the next.

By Sunday, reports of Blossom sightings and interactions made it clear that her network of human friends was growing.

"How's Blossom?" usually started the conversation. They saw her: "She's down the hill."

Then again: "She's up the hill."

Nancy brought over a selfie picture of her and Blossom. Our doe was wearing sunglasses. "I'm still pinching myself that she let me put them on her."

The same day, two little girls reported that they fed her apples that morning. "Our teacher put her picture on the wall in our classroom."

After what felt like an exceptionally long day preparing for the delivery of two hundred bales of hay, I inspected the hayloft with a sense of pride that no amount of grime could diminish. Stale hay and critter nesting debris were replaced by pine shavings' sweet, clean smell. Endless clouds of dust settled slowly back to the floor I just swept. I pulled the hayloft door closed by its rope handle, trying not to look down at the twenty-foot drop to the driveway below.

The ladder in the barn's center aisle was shaky and bent backward on its hinges, like a bad knee joint in need of surgery.

No matter! It was "hot tea time" in the horse barn at Unicorn Hollow. I tossed an apple into each of the five-gallon buckets in front of every stall and filled them with warm water from the hose. The stalls had automatic waterers, but this comforting routine, followed by lots of nickering and splashing, felt more like a treat to close the day on an upbeat note. Justinian especially enjoyed dunking his nose deep in his bucket and blowing bubbles. I think it tickled.

By the time I started for the house, it was dark. A country-living and cricket-noise kind of dark, the latter in roaring form, flapping their crisp wings, or doing whatever it takes to smash those little tambourines on their knees all night—and for what? They'll all end up with bowlegs.

Ha. I can picture it.

Moonbeams cast hues of silver over everything, turning the landscape monochromatic, like old tintype images. Ready for the night, most of the alpacas cushed in cozy pairs, legs were drawn up under their bellies near their shed. Two of my favorites, Tinkerbelle and Royal Velvet, hung out near the fence line, waiting for a treat.

We had what started out to be a perfect evening.

Tonight's meal promised to be "amazing," according to Pino. A bottle of Merlot and a small bouquet of daisies completed his culinary production. We ate by candlelight—the entire room aglow and comfortable. The act of cooking is not only about food and eating to Pino. He goes out of his way to set the stage, ramp up the ambiance, and boost the outcome of the upcoming review of his latest dish.

"Wait a minute." I rearranged and twisted my ponytail into a braid, pulled it to the side, and let it fall over my shoulder. "Voila!" I said. I snapped two daisies from the bouquet, stuck one behind my ear and the other I plaited into the braid. "There ..." I dramatically sipped my wine, shrugged, girly-like, and grinned.

He poured another glass of wine and shifted forward in his chair. "Happy tenth anniversary."

Uh-oh.

"That's next week," I recovered in a flash. "Want to dance?" Life was good.

Squealing tires and popping gravel shattered the serenity and, as if in a slow-motion movie, didn't let up. I shut my eyes, gripped the side of the table, and waited for the inevitable thud of impact. A tree—a deer—Blossom?

Pino was ahead of me. The safety latch clicked, and the heavy door banged into the foyer's wall.

"Blossom!" he yelled.

I grabbed a flashlight from a kitchen drawer, depressed its rubbery switch, and dashed outside, pulling my jacket over one arm. Its feeble beam wavered in my hand, flickered and settled into a steady soft-glowing circle. Wildwood Road appeared deserted. A vague shape near the corner moved. "Pino?"

Over the din of cicadas, a car door slammed. Headlights flashed on-off, on-off as a car turned left, fishtailing up the steep curve of Fox Hill Road. The engine sounded out of sync when the driver changed gears, making a weird *pop-pop-hiss* noise, like a wind-up toy running out of spring.

"Jackass!" Pino shouted.

I glanced at our home, this time with a critical eye. Architectural lace draperies provided the illusion of privacy, but only from the inside. Spying on us would be easy if someone wanted to, as if we lived in a dollhouse, one side wide open.

"No luck," Pino said. "The guy probably skidded out, pulled over, and didn't want to stay around to talk about it. A false alarm. I'll take a look near the pool. She could be hiding." Using the light from his cell phone, he retraced his steps.

The night had a cold inkiness to it, and every deep breath stung my sinuses. Gingerly, I moved forward to the middle of the road, pointing my light close in and as far away as the weak beam would penetrate. The only sounds were crunching gravel under my shoes and the rattle of the clunky flashlight in my shaky hand.

"Blossom, where are you?"

The light picked up a distinct skid-out area on the tar and chip surface, bordered by a curve of splattered gravel. In a direct line, about twenty-five feet off the road, the broad maple, a place between our house and the goings-on around the farm where she liked to go.

Did I imagine a flick of white?

"Aiming my flashlight under the branches, I inched closer, dropped to my knees, and crawled towards Blossom's white hindquarters. She lay on her side, her head propped against the trunk, looking vulnerable and exhausted."

"Pino, over here!"

The faint light was enough to see the obvious pain and bewilderment in Blossom's wide eyes, her mouth opening with each breath. She nuzzled my hand and tried to get up, but her head bumped against one of the limbs. "Hold still ... don't move...." Leaning on one elbow, I examined her face and body as gently as I might touch the wings of a butterfly.

There is a short distance to travel between survival and tragedy. A lucky twist, a split-second delay, a surge of adrenaline. The difference between a bruise and a body that could be snapped like a dry twig. Blossom was lucky: a badly bruised ankle, left knee, and swollen shoulder. Nothing broken. I needed to apply an ice pack to her leg to keep swelling to a minimum. There was no way to know if she had been hit by the car or if she had injured herself trying to get away.

I squeezed my eyes tight and started to stroke the plump, velvety bases of her ears, increasing the pressure toward the furry tips in the acupuncture method of pain control. After a few minutes, she started to relax, and her breathing steadied.

"*Aehh* ..." She turned her head over her bruised shoulder, wedged her right foreleg under her chest, struggling to rock up. She banged her head again.

"*Shhh ... Shhh ...* Wait."

"Was she hit?" Pino brought a rubber mat from the barn. We eased it under her body, then dragged her into the open.

I went to the house for my usual standbys—honey and a little
warm water on her tongue to boost her energy. We helped her
to stand on three legs. She was weary, her ears droopy, her head
barely off the ground. It took another fifteen minutes to help her
into the house.

The injectable pain medication I had for the alpacas worked
well on Blossom. She didn't seem to mind the ice pack on her
shoulder nor the bulky, zebra-patterned vet wrap binding her
ankle. She watched us through half-closed eyes, in and out of
sleep, from a rug in the kitchen. At times, her legs twitched as if
she were still running away. Dreaming, I suppose.

"The driver must have known he hit something. It unnerved
him, so he pulled over." Pino grimaced and tried to make
sense of what had happened.

"But then, how come he didn't say something? First, he hid,
then raced away. A real creep. He could have helped us find her.
Anyway, all I care about is that she's alive."

"She's got to start wearing the reflective orange dog collar
again," Pino said later.

"Too stiff and heavy ... she hates it. Besides, if she gets hung
up on anything, the buckle won't release."

Within days, I started work on a new collar. Blossom still
limped, but not much, and had no trouble getting under tables,
desks, or my piano.

"Blossom move off my foot. I'm getting numb."

"*Aehh* ..." She seemed annoyed at my prodding, shifted her
body slightly, but refused to come out from under the sewing
table. The familiar electric hum of the sewing machine and a
surge of power jerked the fabric and my fingers toward the needle assembly.

"*Yeow!*" I yanked my hands away. That was dangerous. I
brought the foot pedal closer, straightened the power cord, and
got back to work. The machine surged again.

"Blossom, NO!" I pushed her head away from the pedal and pulled the connecting wire from under her leg.

"Almost done." I flipped the machine's guide foot in place and continued to sew the two-tricolor, fluorescent athletic armbands together, adding a piece of Velcro for a closure. My design was lightweight, flexible, and reflective—perfect for a collar that would not come off on its own but could break away if she got hung up on something.

"Come out, Blossom. People will be able to see you better now." Pleased with my design, I tugged and tested the collar's strength. "Where's my model?"

With a grunt, she crawled from under the worktable, yawned, and bowed into an enviable body stretch that must have realigned her vertebrae from neck to tail. I patted her rump.

"Now, when people see you, they'll know somebody loves you."

She sniffed the collar hanging from my wrist; I slipped it over her snout. She let it dangle a long time before tossing it off.

"Come on, let me see how you look in your lucky rainbow collar." I fastened it around her neck and fussed over her like a little girl flaunting a new petticoat. Her tail wagged nonstop.

"You're a razzle-dazzle, baby!" I exclaimed and clapped my hands at the success of my design. "Let's get a picture."

I held the viewing screen of my Canon camera for Pino. "So, what do you think of this picture? I was thinking of putting together some sort of advertising. A 'Protect Blossom' campaign. You know, with posters, and maybe try for some press coverage."

Pino studied the photo. "Her ears look too big. Angle the shot a little and center the collar." He made a raspberry sound to get her attention. Blossom turned and looked straight into the camera.

Shh ... click ... "Got it."

Two days later, I carried the heavy box of newly minted posters into the office. As if they were a long-awaited present, I cut the tape and flipped back the lid.

Blossom's face radiated youth and vigor in the image, her eyes bright and curious. Bold lettering read, "Please Don't Shoot Blossom, We Love Her." It was a simple invitation, asking for a chance to explain the favor I asked of our community.

What else could I do but start the conversation? I didn't know what to expect, but I did hope somebody would question my audacity to ask that they consider Blossom—who she is, what she means to us—before they try to kill her.

"Thought we decided on a dozen." Pino held one eighteen-inch poster up to the light. "The shop did a good job laminating them." He ran his fingers along the edges. "How many did you buy?" He put the poster on top of the foot-high pile.

"Fifty." I flashed him with a self-satisfied grin. "What? They ran a special. I hope adding our 800-phone number was a smart move."

Armed with a hammer, a pack of wire staples, and a load of posters, we began what was to be a never-ending campaign.

Protecting Blossom.

Chapter 8

Our Mission

Hundreds of sharp-eyed blackbirds searched for the last of the dogwood berries, some of them diving into leafy mounds in search of the few that got away.

Pino, with Caruso on his shoulder, Blossom, Kaya, and I were an oddball family of motley players who brought smiles and a sense of healthy kookiness to our community. Crunching through windblown piles of dried autumn leaves along the roads around Unicorn Hollow, we hung our picture posters in the most visible locations—as though, by doing that, we could keep her safe.

Or the plan could backfire.

We hoped our optimism would be contagious, especially when linked to our sweet young doe who promised friendship in exchange for a kindly pat. Every landowner within a mile radius of our farm now knew of our campaign to protect Blossom and was asked, begged, and cajoled to spread the word and spare the deer with the rainbow collar.

"Come meet Blossom and bring your camera," I would say. "We Have fresh-baked cookies for the kids. We live close by— over the river and through the woods." Most were surprised, a few polite but non-committal, while others had heard about Blossom and were happy to spread the word and help.

One landowner asked, "Who could possibly want to kill such a lovely animal?"

A few people, apparently. They flat-out said they would.

I always hoped that they had gotten it wrong, that they would think about it, and change their minds. Those were the times I relied heaviest on Pino's support and the simplest gesture of holding his hand to lift my spirits.

I psyched myself for today's visit to Cloverdale Farm, the last boundary farm on our list. The morning was full of promise. I raised the thermostat in my car and dropped the mirrored visor. *So much for dollin' up.* A comb, lipstick, and a touch of powder to cut the shine. That and a John Denver song was my quick remedy for a mental tune-up.

"Country roads—take me home ..." I tried to yodel like my bird, Caruso, and headed down Fox Hill Road in what we had defined as Blossom's territory. Before long, I was following a split rail fence along Homestead Road and pulled into a driveway with broad sweeping curves. At the entrance, "Welcome to Cloverdale Farm" was carved into a wood sign above the painting of a fox.

I slowed to a stop, opened my window, and gazed at the pastoral setting nestled beneath the baby-blue sky. *On days like these, the air smells clean and sweet.* Resting my head on my arm, I let the early sun warm my face and looked at the horses grazing their way across a field.

It only got better. Easing off the break, I continued to a spot where a stream meandered beneath old granddaddy oaks, tumbled over bulbous, moss-laden rocks, and tugged at the sun on its journey to a pond situated at the far end of a white two-story house. Then, a flock of Canada geese swooped low over the roof, squawking as geese do, gliding in, pivoting feet-first at the last second to a smooth water landing.

Beyond the final curve, a woman was stacking decorative dried grasses in a tall wicker basket. Next to her stood a tiny, black Jack Russell terrier, no bigger than eight-pound Kaya. I parked, made my way toward her, and smiled before introducing myself.

Later that same day, I remembered how the conversation effortlessly flowed. Her name was Jeanne. She was poised, friendly, and sparkled with curiosity.

"What 'cha got there?" She smiled.

I showed her a poster and a photo of Kaya happily licking Blossom's face.

"She's no bigger than Bear," Jeanne said. "Hi, Bear." I bent to the tiny dog.

She took a poster and studied it. "Where did you find the fawn? Where is she now?"

As I talked, I started to re-live the adventure of raising Blossom. "She's funny, considerate—always unexpected—always a surprise.

"There are times when I feel a mental connectedness with her. I know where she is, even though it seems impossible. Saying it sounds crazy, but I can't deny the feeling."

I told her how Blossom interacted with people and mirrored our actions since babyhood—how she took pleasure in the tiniest flowers and about the unlikely things that interested her, "like the wallpaper in our den."

"Wallpaper?"

"The textured pattern scratches her nose. She scoots back- ward, butt high, tail fluttering, and gives that wall a mischievous, squinty-eyed look, and then darts back and forth like she's discovered a new plaything." I hopped around to demonstrate. "*Boing ... boing.*"

Bear spun, backed up, and barked.

Jeanne pointed at the little dog. "Like that?" Her voice was full of fun and laughter. She hopped on one leg. "Or, like this?" An ear-to-ear grin beamed across her face.

I should have left my doubts at home.

"I jog up Fox Hill often. Can I drop in to visit you soon and meet Blossom?"

"Please do!"

True to her word, a few days later, Jeanne jogged up our hill and came for a visit. She carried a backpack with her camera.

I sat on a large boulder on our front lawn, grooming Blossom and sharing a bag of vegetable chips with her while our new friend peeked from behind the long lens of her Nikon. She crouched for a low-angle shot—the shutter whined, two clicks at a time.

"The deer on our farm are still shedding, but you're as silky and shiny as a new penny," she told Blossom. "So, young lady, what's your secret?" She snapped another picture. "She's so well-bred. Polite, a real class act."

I felt proud. It was true. Blossom's tawny coat reflected light, like heavy Asian silk. "Her biggest secret is that she lives with someone who brushes her every day." I pulled a few strands of hair from her brush. "Under my microscope, this hair appears smooth, like hollow rods. See for yourself, go ahead, roll it between your fingers. It's her climate control."

Jeanne examined the hair. "Feels like plastic. No frizzy hair days for you, huh?" For the third time, she paused to clean the smudge marks on her camera lens. "You're funny." She tweaked Blossom's nose.

"I was thinking ... this is all perfectly reasonable," Jeanne said. "One, you show her unconditional love and caring, three squares a day—plus junk food." She clucked her disapproval. "And two, you play with her as if she were a domesticated animal. It shouldn't be all that shocking that some dormant personality gene activated, and she bloomed into Miss Congeniality."

Blossom loved crunchy veggie chips and shoved her face into the loudest crackling bag on the planet. I pulled the bag away. "One chip for you—one chip for me."

"I see it, but I don't believe it." Jeanne's camera captured the moment.

Shh ... click, shh ... click.

The three of us headed for the house. "Come on; I want you to see the holiday antlers I made."

"Antlers, for a doe?"

"She likes to wear it. Wait, you'll see."

Blossom's feet tapped across the slate floor toward the basket of her stuff we kept next to a low console table in the foyer. An ornate, rectangular mirror hung above the table. We called it Blossom's Looking Glass.

I didn't tell Jeanne what might happen next.

"*Aehh* ..." Blossom nosed the decorated headband. A star- burst tiara covered with aluminum foil lay on top of a miniature cloth doll she got tired of dragging around the house. I untangled strands of the doll's curly hair from a silvery ribbon, brushed it off, and fit the headband in front of Blossom's ears.

"Wait," I whispered.

The fancy mirror did justice to this particular girl's feminine psyche as she contemplated her image, turning this way and that, her eyes always remaining focused on her face.

"She likes hats?"

"There are always wet nose and lick marks to wipe off the mirror. She's been strutting and clowning around like that since her fawn days."

Just then, Blossom flipped her head and sent the antler-tiara flying into the living room.

"Vanity, thy name is woman—in any species," Jeanne said. Later, we carried hot mugs of tea, biscotti, and a bowl of cherries to the patio. And so, bundled in puffy jackets against a nip in the air, we took turns offering cherries to the doe curled next to the table. Before long, Blossom yawned, got up, and moseyed down the stone steps toward the garden.

Jeanne shoved a lock of shiny dark hair behind her ear and gazed at me. "Just like a fairytale. I have a story to tell you."

I leaned forward, my fingers laced around one knee. "I'm ready."

Her dark eyes turned serious, lost in thought. "Last month I saw a red-tailed hawk shot right out of the sky. It was terrible. Two of them were soaring above my pasture when I heard the gunshot. One bird stalled, fluttering in a lopsided spiral—the other bird screeching and diving close enough to touch its wounded companion—then flew away. The wounded bird thumped to the ground and tried to right itself.

"I ran to help it. At the same time, a man jumped from the top rail of my fence, holding a shotgun over his head in one hand. He moved fast, like an athlete. 'Don't touch my bird,' he was shouting."

She paused and wrapped her hands around the warm mug. "I ran, hands out front, palms open. 'No, no, no, you don't. Stop! Get off my land!'"

"He shouted back, 'What's your problem, lady? I shot that bird. He's mine.'"

"You must have been terrified," I said.

"Not yet. At first, I was just annoyed." She dunked the biscotti ferociously in her tea and tapped it against the cup.

"It was what happened next that I can't get out of my mind. The hawk was still alive and had stretched one wing out for balance, each brown-pointed flight feather on its left wing perfect.

The other wing was blood-soaked and red, like the color of its tail.

"The hunter took another step closer and reached for the hawk.

"'Don't touch that bird.' I moved between him and the bird and got my cell phone out of my pocket. 'I'm calling the police.'

"He looked startled. And that's when he swung the gun in my direction."

"No! Straight at you? Crazy." My jaw dropped.

"Not straight at my belly, but a threatening move, none-the-less. I thought about backing off. But then I saw the hawk looking at me as if it wondered why it was still alive. Who knows? Maybe it realized I would defend it. But, at that moment, that defenseless bird gave me the courage to stand up to the hunter."

The story absorbed her; her lips tightened, and her hands curled into fists on the table.

She lowered her voice and said the words slowly and deeply. "'Don't you dare threaten me with your big gun, buddy. You're trespassing. Besides, you just broke the law by shooting a red-tailed hawk. Get the hell off my land.'" Jeanne cocked her arm at the elbow and swung it out to demonstrate. "And ... then, I reached out and pushed the gun barrel away from me."

By that time, I had both hands pressed against my face. "You pushed the gun away?"

"So, what else could I have done? Blubber like a wimp and run home crying? I don't think so."

"What about the hawk? Did he take the bird?"

She was surprised that I would even suggest it. "You're kidding, right? No way would I let him take that poor bird, dead or alive. I mean, he shot into the pasture where my horses were grazing and tried to intimidate me with his friggin' gun!" She paused and took a deep breath. "He's the one who took a hike."

"Good for you. Geez, you've got guts."

She shook her head. "I don't think bravery had much to do with it. Remember, he had a gun. Later, I thought about what happened and how dumb I was to push the gun barrel away." She groaned. "What if it had gone off? I was too angry to be smart."

"What about the bird? Did it die?"

"Nope." Her mouth twisted into a sly grin. "Recovering nicely at a raptor sanctuary, thank you." She lifted her mug. "Here's to one brave bird. He's got a splint on his wing, but the vet says he'll fly again."

"What about the hunter?"

"As of today, he's got real problems with our neighbors for shooting a hawk and hunting without permission."

The look of concern and the words she said next sent a shiver of fear up my spine.

"Annie, I'm worried about your safety. Be cautious in what you're doing when you're trying to protect Blossom. If this can happen to me, while trying to protect a bird, imagine what can happen when you're trying to protect a deer."

I haven't been called Annie since I was little.

She fumbled through her backpack and found a small notepad. "Last night, I wrote a poem about the hawk. Want to hear it?"

I nodded.

THE HAWK

Whenever I weigh the cost of love,
the shattered heart, and senseless pain
I remember the wounded hawk,
his wing held out like a beggar.
And how I with reckless abandon
gathered up his terrible beauty
just to hold for one moment
something as wild and free as love.

Chapter 9

The Oldwick General Store

It was all about rich, aromatic coffee, country cooking, and breakfast in town on Sundays. Eggs, from pampered hens, over light, not gooky—crisp ham, home fries, and freshly baked zucchini bread.

The aged and warped wooden porch of the Oldwick General Store creaked underfoot with typical turn-of-the-century charm. Decorated "his" and "her" corn brooms jutted bottom-side-up from a weathered whiskey barrel.

Someone creative had tucked hair of curled-wood shavings demurely under "her" giant sunflower hat and pasted a red twine-stitched smile under huge black button eyes. Beneath a jaunty fedora, the obvious "he" of the duo welcomed all with the wavy string smirk of a scarecrow.

I imagined stores were like this in the early 1900s in Gardner, Massachusetts, where my mother grew up. Then too, their general store doubled as a gathering place where she and her friends met, shared news, and gossip went wild. She kept those pictures in a keepsake box. I remember ribboned pigtails, Mom holding hands with her best friend Happy, in front of a counter of soaps and candy rolls in waxed paper. Next to them were two barrels, one for pickles and another with a selection of straw brooms.

Pino opened the clunky old screen door, and I followed him inside, carrying a poster I wanted to tack on the community bulletin board. Thick, rusting springs slammed the door behind me.

Bang!

I jumped, glanced around, embarrassed that I hadn't remembered about the door, like a newbie to the area.

The place was eclectic, to say the least. Framed prints of the neighboring towns of Tewksbury, Oldwick, and Bedminster lined every pastel-washed wall. "God Bless" this and that signs, paraphernalia, and a conglomeration of antique, high-button shoes dangled from laces tied over hand-hewn timbers.

"I'm going to buy some zucchini bread," Pino said, waving to Steve, the deli proprietor.

"How's your deer?" Steve called out kindly.

"She's wonderful, thanks." I headed toward the aisle of daily roasted brewed coffees.

My favorite table was open, a cozy spot near the original stacked stone fireplace. I sat at the edge of a stiff-backed wicker chair, felt the cup's warmth, and sipped a hot cinnamon flavored latte. As usual, my gaze lingered on the fox hunting print hanging above the mantle. The picture conjured up enough detail to scare the dickens out of anyone thinking of trying the sport.

Powerful horses, men in scarlet jackets and women riding sidesaddle in flowing skirts, all in top hats—galloping, jumping hedges, some with eyes popping in terror, hanging on for dear life, others crashing. Hounds scattered, continuing to watch the fiasco from behind a hedgerow.

From another area, separated by a wide pass-through, the robust guffaws of three men rebounded around the room. A heavyset man, the center of attention within the party of three, pumped one hand to emphasize the conversation while his other hand deftly squirted ketchup on his food.

"Forget the Blossom burgers," he laughed in a breathy chuckle. "I can't wait to get my hands on a big, fat ole Blossom steak. Fellas, we're gonna have a feast. I made a bullet with that doe's name on it." He patted the denim pocket over his heart and choked on his laughter. I instantly despised him.

My face felt red hot. Without thinking much about what I would do, I gripped the table's edge, pushed my chair back, and stood. It made an awful grating sound on the broad planks. Diners stared, their easy morning chatter stalled. An elderly woman put her hand to her throat in a universal "Are you choking?" question to me. Even the fat guy who joked about killing Blossom was paying attention.

Something ... say something ... anything.

As if I swallowed the words, I couldn't speak. "*Why do you want to kill my Blossom?*" I wanted to yell, but couldn't. I stood, rigid—my breath stuck on pause—too frozen by anger, indecision, and an undercurrent of fear. The sentence "I made a bullet with that doe's name on it" replayed its horror on a voice loop in my mind. The words hovered in my open mouth—I almost got the courage.

Almost.

"Anna." Pino placed the package of bread on the table, brushed his hand over mine, and stretched out his arms to hug me. "Remember the swan?"

Ah, yes, the swan. In theory, our made-up iconic swan was supposed to allow provocation about Blossom to roll off my back, like water rolls off the back of a swan. At least to me, it was clear that my swan had flown the coop—with the chickens.

"You want to move to another room?"

I sat down, no longer interested in breakfast. "Pino, they're going to shoot Blossom, and eat her!"

Steve came from behind the counter, wiping his hands on a long white chef's apron. He smiled warmly. "Sorry about that. Don't let those guys worry you. Let's see the picture."

I removed the rubber band and flattened the poster on the table.

"Is this for me?" In high spirits, he picked it up. "I'll be right back. Want to show some of the fellas our town's favorite deer." He walked into the next room, pulled out a chair, and joined the men. I saw them lean in and gawk at the picture. They all laughed.

And then they didn't.

The man in the bib overalls looked uncomfortable. He lifted his meaty face toward us and nodded. His apologetic look was unmistakable.

Pino waved in return.

Steve came back to our table. "What did you say?" Pino asked.

"Nothing much, I thought they should know that you're the people who raised the deer they're joking about. Locals, a bunch of old-timers, having fun with the idea of a tame deer. They didn't know about you, or they wouldn't have acted like such asses." He waved to his assistant Al, who stood behind the glass deli counter. Steve held up the poster. "What do you think? Okay for the bulletin board?"

Al nodded with an enthusiastic thumbs-up and moved a few flyers and a handful of business cards to the edges of the cork-board. An older man walked over to us, thumped his hand on Steve's back, and cocked his head toward Blossom's poster.

"I'd like to meet that gal," he snickered and punched his finger at the picture. "Damned good lookin' doe. I heard the talk," he said. "There's a guy comes in here from Texas who has one of these pictures hanging on his trophy wall, between two big-time bucks. One of my boys told me."

"On the wall?" Pino asked.

"Seems likely that it's better than her head, don't you think?" He smiled slightly and nodded. "I lived here fifty years. They won't hurt your young doe." He looked pointedly at the men in the adjoining room.

"You going to tell them not to?" Pino followed his gaze. "Already have." The old man's eyes swept back to the table of men. "They're my kids." He gave a little laugh. "Hey, Steve. When are you going to open for supper?"

"Soon as I can count on more than only you showing up." He turned back to the register, clearly enjoying the banter.

"Thank you," I said to Steve, kissing his cheek before we left. "No problem, my friends."

The church bell signaled the end of services at the white clapboard Zion Lutheran Church across Main Street, and Oldwick started to bustle with activity. Groups of smiling parishioners gathered around the pastor, while others walked arm-in-arm toward the General Store.

Perfect timing.

Our "Please Don't Shoot Blossom" poster quickly drew attention. Within a day, Steve phoned with an update—a few personal fan notes, some by children, were written on the poster. A few comments tacked to the bulletin board were not so nice. Steve added, "You'll like most of them."

"Most of them?" I contemplated why I dared think this would be easy.

Later that evening, one of our friends, Jeff, called to ask what we thought of the hunting article in Saturday's Weekender section. Last week's local newspaper article was familiar and particularly loathsome to me. It featured a highly coiffed, camo-suited woman, a rakish scarf flung over her shoulder, her head high, chin up, gun poised. Her hair was lacquered, and her makeup perfect.

The quote read, "I only shoot what I can eat." I bit my lip at her arrogance and lack of empathy.

How couldn't they see?

Not one word about the once vibrant young buck, now dead, on which her fancy boot comfortably rested. In my eyes, that was the real story. I wished someone would have cared enough to close the buck's eyes and put his tongue back in his mouth so that he, too, could pose with the illusion of dignity. The message was clear.

It was fashionable to kill.

Pino snapped me back to the present. "I told Jeff about your conversation with the editor. He thinks we're making a huge mistake by taking Blossom's story public." He squeezed my hand. "Damn, I don't know whether to be upset or relieved by the publicity. Getting involved in controversy is always a double-edged sword. Maybe we should re-think this."

Why was he caving? I tried to keep the disappointment out of my voice. "Oh, for God's sake. Then, we have to create more."

"What?"

"Choices."

Chapter 10

Notoriety

This meeting could be a mistake. Burdened by doubt, I took a deep breath, held it, exhaled through pressed lips, and opened the door for the reporter.

"Anna? Hi, I'm Maude Kenyon." A lady with mischievous eyes extended her hand and focused on me over the rim of tortoise-shell glasses.

We connected; I liked her right away. She turned to a slim young man in his mid-thirties coming up the steps, holding a tripod, bag, and camera with a lens the size of a magnum bottle of wine. "Meet Tim, my photographer."

He noticed my interest, cocked his head to one side, shared a smile, and tapped the lens protectively. "My baby."

Just inside the door, Maude hesitated, raised an eyebrow, and chuckled. "Oh, my God! This is hard to believe ... Tim, would you look at that?"

He was all action and snapped several pictures of Blossom before he had a chance to take the camera bag over his shoulder. Maude sounded business-like and not surprised, although she must have been.

For support, I reached back and let my hand rest lightly on Blossom's forehead. I was counting on Maude's judgment as a well-respected, issue-oriented reporter.

"Meet my baby," I said.

Blossom followed us outside, her feet clicking like tap shoes on the stone patio. The day was hot, mid-eighties, but thankfully not humid. That morning, Pino had set a small writing table next to a semi-circular seating area in the garden. It was cooler under the poplars and inviting. I fluffed up the new cushions made of a pretty chintz fabric; bold flowers scattered over a black background.

Maude observed the animals and landscape: the alpacas watching, always curious, Justinian neighing to one of the horses, and a couple of joggers coming up Fox Hill Road. She relaxed and poured herself a drink of iced lemonade. I had a separate cup of ice cubes for Blossom.

We were quiet and let Blossom weave in and around the chairs like it was no big deal to share our time with a wild deer. I snuck Tim a few carrots to feed her. He allowed her to poke at his camera.

Maude hesitated and launched into the conversation in a matter-of-fact tone. "I've been giving her angle a lot of thought."

Her *angle*? Startled by the word, I felt vulnerable; my wall of anxieties closed in as if I had betrayed a confidence or gotten caught passing secrets to the enemy. Blossom's existence was on a need-to-know basis until now. I imagined radical, angry people who would grope a newspaper story for the coordinates to track her down.

Would she understand? *I need more time. I'll apologize for their time and trouble.*

Maude leaned toward me, touched my arm, and shook it slightly. "Worry will wear you down. Leave it to me. A good number of people will want to help." She took my hand to comfort me. It mattered.

"Do you want to get your message out? Yes? No? Sort of?" she asked with a wry grin. "You'll see, it can turn her into a cause to celebrate."

"That obvious, huh?" I tried to clear my mind and expand my thinking. "I'm worried about the downside of publicity, sorry." She paid attention to my reactions as I talked, building the depth of Blossom's story with her questions. And, with not much more effort, she gave me something to hope for as a glint of sun shined through a crack in a cloud. Anything was possible.

"Give me a moment," Maude said.

I left to check on one of our pregnant female alpacas, China. Her baby would be huge, which is always a worry. Blossom seemed happy with her new friends.

I was still close.

Tim started shooting pictures, scooting back and forth. Twisting the camera from horizontal to vertical, he kissed at the air and waved to the sky to keep Blossom's attention fixed on him. "That's it ... here, Blossom." She knew this type of give-and-take play and lowered her head to her shoulder and, in her shy way, raised her eyes to him. He snapped the picture. "I think I'm in love," he laughed.

Our lilacs and roses were in full bloom next to the patio. I saw Maude looking up into the leafy canopy, turning to follow a fragrance to a row of lilacs on the far side of the patio. She glanced at her watch, slowly sipped lemonade, then got back to work, contemplating—her head pivoted on her fist, looking between Blossom, the photographer, and her writing. She jabbed the pen decisively at her notebook for another hour, leaned back, and finished.

The day had been perfect—leafy shadows elongated in the late afternoon sun. As I topped the hill from the barn, I could see Pino making his way toward Maude, balancing a tray of cheese and grapes in one hand, a bottle of wine gripped in the other.

Maude lifted her eyebrows, her eyes defiant. "Did you read about the lawsuit against the town council of Princeton?

Dreadful. How the Mayor dared allow a private hunting group to bait, net, and deadbolt deer in the park—even the fawns screamed." She twisted in her chair, trying to shake the thought. "One Princeton resident called it a 'barbaric slaughter.'" She slapped her hands on her knees and shook her head in disbelief.

"Yeah, we know," I said. We heard about it through an online club called Friends of Deer. Know what? Never in my life have I never thought about joining any group of activists, much less going on a march to protest. But this feels right … they have enough spunk to make a difference. I'm going to make a sign to carry. What do you think? If we can find enough empathy for Blossom, raise awareness in this group—?"

"There's a lot of conversation about an alternative, humane method of contraception," Pino added. "A vaccine we can give Blossom."

"Only for Blossom?" Maude said with a rueful smile. "Isn't the point to benefit all deer?" She made another note. "I agree. Either way, you're smart to begin with a soft protest."

Maude stood, her long flowery skirt billowing in a puff of breeze. Blossom had been grazing nearby and jerked to attention.

"*Aehh* …"

I saw that certain look, that certain tilt of her head, the jump of joy when something triggered her playful nature, in this case, Maude's skirt.

"Uh-oh." Pino stepped in to block her.

"No, no, I'm fine." Maude jigged away with the exuberance of a youngster. Gathering her skirt, she hid behind me, urging Blossom to play. Kaya came over to join in peek-a-boo.

"I can't stand it," Maude said, laughing. "You're wearing me out!" Maude was huffing when she returned, sat down, and reached for the wine. "Whew! So, now I guess we're buddies," she said and offered the deer an ice cube.

Maude pointed at Blossom, scribbled another note, and let her pen linger over the page. "This story has teeth, a life of its own. There are enough people around here who feel the same as you, but they're not able to pull at the heartstrings of the community—like she can. She's beautiful, gentle, and ..."—she wiggled her fingers in the air— "has a touch of fantasy about her."

★ ★ ★

"PLEASE DON'T SHOOT BLOSSOM," headlined the half-page story and picture in July's *Weekender,* Hunterdon's county-wide newspaper.

Maude's clever article recounted the story of her introduction to the little deer who had revealed another side of nature to our community, weaving in the reasons why it would be so easy to love and want to protect her. She wrote with humor of her urge to "burp" the young doe after feeding her a bottle of milk: *I'm a sucker for babies. So, when I met Blossom, I oohed and aahed...*

She captured and acknowledged what the hunting facet of her audience would think and might say. During the interview, Blossom walked over twice and stuck her nose into the plastic glass of lemonade. Not that she had a thing for anything sugary, it was the ice cubes she was after. No doubt about it—Maude was smitten.

It's hard to believe until you meet her, she wrote.
"We don't want to infringe on others' rights," Pino was quoted.
"We're simply asking people to let us protect this one deer."
She's one of the unmentionables. You know her kind. They eat your shrubs and flowers, even those on the list of things

they're believed to avoid. Even worse, they eat the farmers'
crops causing real economic hardship. There must be some way
to save this outgoing, friendly doe.

It didn't take long to get a response from the article. Digital
clocks never let you forget the exact time. It was 2:53 a.m. when
the phone rang.

It's always bad news if it comes in the middle of the night.
"Turn on the speakerphone," I whispered, rolling on my
forearm.

The caller was shouting and growling over a low-level squeal
of background noise. He sounded furious. "What the hell do
you think you're doing with that deer? I'll tell you what—she's
gonna be dead meat! Nobody tells me what to do."

Okay—so a few words about Pino and his Italian heritage
from Sicily. I could almost hear the blood churning, his anger
rising, and the measured space between his thoughts and spoken
words.

"Go to hell! Do you think that calling in the middle of the
night to threaten us makes you special, a big guy with a gun?
Act like a human being, for God's sake!"

No response. I thought the caller had hung up.

The person cleared his throat. "I know where she is," came
the threatening words, stunning in their finality. After a long
pause, the phone clicked off.

"What now?" I stared at the phone, expecting it to jump to
life on its own.

Pino was quiet, an uncharacteristic scowl set on his face.
"Not all the monkeys are in the zoo. He's taking this as a personal affront to his right to hunt."

I hoped the surge of helplessness would go away. It didn't. It
was too late.

Chapter 11

Confrontation

As the days turned noticeably shorter, and nature's hues of gold and crimson lit up the landscape, artificial DayGlo safety vests became mandatory apparel for lots of jittery people around Tewksbury.

During hunting season, man's intrusion in nature did not go unnoticed.

Mary flew in from Miami to help choose which alpacas we would take to the annual breeder's exposition the next month in Pennsylvania. Tinkerbelle was a champion, on a winning streak for her silky fleece and conformation. I chuckled at the thought of my sister taking center stage, hamming it up in the spotlight, while the stunning animal paraded in the arena looking like a puffy piñata.

We waited for Sunday, the only no-hunting day in New Jersey, to enjoy a long, leisurely trail ride. Many months had gone by since we last enjoyed the quiet time that comes with riding—the rhythmic movement of a horse, a gulp of warmed spiced cider from a leather Bota bag slung over my shoulder, and the serenity that allowed normally guarded feelings and opinions to flow in effortless

Identical twins such as Mary and I looked so much alike that it was sometimes freaky-funny. I remember one instance, trying on similar hats in front of neck-height back-to-back mirrored vanities at Macy's. I thought I was admiring myself. Spookier still, Mary didn't realize that it was me she was smiling at until I moved away from the mirror, and "her" head disappeared! Our laughter was infectious; those shoppers around us who witnessed the twin surprise moment shared in the laughter.

"Off with her head," Mary had shouted, slicing her hand across her throat. We had such fun being twins, and yet, I often wondered about the disruption in our lives and how she coped with abandonment when I was rushed to the hospital. All the hugging in the world could not explain away trauma to a one-year-old. She grew up in the turmoil of our home. I sometimes thought I was the lucky one.

It was mid-afternoon before we finished grooming and saddling Justinian and Simba. "Put this reflective band on your helmet," I said, straightening the matching vest of fluorescent fabric over her jacket.

I stayed at Simba's head while Mary stepped on the mounting block and climbed into the saddle. She made a face and pulled at the armhole of her safety vest. "I am ... just brilliant! Does this thing flash?"

"Pull the cord in your pocket, "I joked, mounted Justinian. "C'mon, you can be honest. You said that Sundays are 'no hunting' days. Right?" She coaxed me with a nod to agree before gathering Simba's reins and following me out the gates. "I'll never learn. All I want is a quiet ride." She sighed. "I have a bad feeling about this."

"Ah, so now you're psychic?"

"Always have been." She inclined her head, unsure.

We crossed the dent in the hill that was Wildwood Road, following a steep, haphazard deer trail to the massive granite outcropping facing our farm, then to an old stone wall not far from Blossom's den. The air smelled of dried leaves and dirt.

Typical of this time of year, winds kept the ground dry, and abundant wildflowers grew, following the sun across the sky.

At first, it was difficult to see into the shadows. But hanging out with Blossom had taught me how to focus beyond the light and recognize the intricate subtleties of shaded detail— the topline of a back, the flick of an ear, a shudder, a raised leg. Standing high in my stirrups, I could see several deer camouflaged in their surroundings until they, too, became obvious.

"Blossom."

She started toward us.

I dismounted and waited for the inevitable lick. "Hi, sweet girl. Look a' you." Her undercoat had grown in thick, a forecast of the cold winter to come. I loosened her collar and spent a few minutes scratching the flattened hair underneath. She pawed at the broad base of a tree, nibbling at a tuft of grass that had survived the cold snap.

"You stay here with your friends." I stepped on a downed tree trunk, jammed my foot in the stirrup, and swung my leg over the saddle.

A gentle thrill of affection welled up when I looked back and saw the silhouette of Blossom on a small mound of earth, watching our progress. I turned so Mary could hear me over the crackle of dried vegetation. "Sometimes I feel as if I'm living a dream. It's only that ..." I faltered; it was hard to explain. "I try to hold tight to every moment with her. More moments to make more memories."

"Will she follow us?"

"I don't think so. Animals are wary during hunting season. Not only people get jumpy."

"Yeah, Sis, I know. We're all worried."

We crossed upper Fox Hill Road to the first of several fields boxed in by streams and bridle paths.

"How's your farm search in Virginia going?" Mary had been looking for a farm for almost two years. From California to New Mexico, Massachusetts to Florida. Every farm turned out to be either too old, too big, too overgrown, too flat.

"I'll let you know next week. You and Pino have to move too, so we can all be together?" She always asked, knowing the probable answer. As her farm search progressed, so did the realization that we couldn't—would not—leave Blossom behind.

A branch snapped, well off to the side. Justinian spun toward the sound, his eyes locked on the trees, his ears pointed like daggers at the perceived danger. He snorted, once, twice—as loud as steam chugging from a locomotive. I could feel his heart pounding through the saddle.

I reined him in. "Whoa!" My left foot lost its toehold, one safety breakaway stirrup released, and I slid, grabbing for his mane and the ridge of his neck, slippery with sweat. "Justinian ... whoa." I pulled myself back in the saddle.

Mary came alongside with Simba. "You okay? Could it be an animal?"

"Wait."

I bent over his mane. Using Justinian's ears as guideposts of sorts, I scanned the woods. Concealed behind the leafy shield was something else. An unexpected movement, out of sync with its surroundings, and a face, half-hidden behind the telescopic sight of a rifle.

Never had I seen someone aim a real gun at me. Growing up, kids knew not to point toy guns, even if you were playing cowboys and waving a plastic gun in the air. Rules ruled. Back then. It was a matter of right and wrong.

"I give up," I yelled, raising my hands to the hunter. Mary leaned over. "Who are you surrendering to?"

I pointed. "Over there." Even as I said it, the knot in my stomach tightened. "In that tree, a guy—with a gun."

The rifle lowered. The hunter seemed to grin before training the gun in our direction again.

Breathe—deep breath in—long breath out.

"I see him!" Mary's voice hissed in a too-tight throat.

"Git away," the voice behind the gun boomed. "You cost me the buck I spent all day waitin' for. Git outta here!"

Mary and I looked at each other with understanding. "No problem; we're going," I called.

He didn't answer. A leafy branch moved aside, and I glimpsed the rifle again, this time its barrel used as a directional signal. His not-so-vague threat stunned me. I remembered Jeanne's words, and the "don't you dare touch that bird, buddy" follow-up when she protected the hawk.

My courage made a slow comeback.

"Maybe you should be the one leaving. These are public trails, and I assume you know about no hunting on Sundays?"

"Git outta here."

"And stop pointing that damn gun at us." Mary was angry. "Do you have permission to be up there with a gun?"

"Nice touch, Sis!" I muttered under my breath. "Shush!"

"The bully who shouts loudest backs down pretty fast, if you call them on it," Mary said, with a whole lot of confidence. Most likely, she was faking.

"We're out of here. A steady easy trot."

"No sense arguing with someone with a gun," Mary agreed.

Could we pull this off without falling?

"I'm ready." Mary made soothing sounds to Simba, stroked his chestnut coat, now streaked dark with rivulets of sweat.

Being helpless in the crosshairs felt sickening. My back tingled with a raw, almost unbearable sensation as I imagined something vile and invisible creeping up behind us. It didn't matter if it was legal or not—evil or not. The threat was real.

Ever since we were kids, we chatted, joked, and laughed in tense situations, a sort of equalizing tactic that probably has a legitimate diagnosis in some psychological journal. Or, it might be a twin thing.

"Tell me, Sis," I said. "Do you remember the time we were walking off-shore in Key Biscayne, and the police helicopter swooped low over us, trying to divert the sharks in the area? You thought the cops liked your new bikini?"

She glanced up quickly, surprised. "Yeah."

"Remember how I kept telling you how glad I was that you were there with me because there was a fifty-fifty chance that the sharks would get you first?"

"*Hmmm* ... it's been a long time. You're sure it wasn't my bikini?" Mary asked.

I tried to sound casual but talked to her sharply. "So, Mary Canary, I'm sorry to have to tell you that this is another one of those times."

After a nervous laugh, she frowned, just like in the old days.

Boom, boom, boom. Fast and explosive, not the crack I would have expected from a hunting rifle.

My hands quivered through the reins, directly to Justinian's sensitive mouth. He responded with a rumbling, anxious whinny followed by jerky sidesteps.

"Up ahead, just beyond the bend—a shortcut to the right. Make sure to keep your knees tucked tight. The horses know these trails."

"But, why did he shoot? He can see we're leaving." Mary's eyes were wide with fear, and the shaky death grip she had on the reins was all-telling.

I couldn't ride far enough to escape what must have happened.

"He's not after us. It's probably the buck."

"But, still ..."

"There it is," I said. The deer path was obvious, once you knew it was there. We trotted single file through a stand of birch trees, down a short slope of high grasses, and walked into the stream. The danger had passed, no need to hurry. The stream glistened. I let the reins slip through my fingers as cold mountain water swished around Justinian's ankles. Justinian and Simba nuzzled each other, lowered their heads, and drank.

"You did a good job with Simba. You okay?"

"Just terrific. You did say a quiet ride?" Mary made a face. "Maybe next time we'll wear bulletproof vests."

"Think of the positives. No sharks."

In less than a half-hour, we re-crossed Fox Hill Road. I scanned the woods for Blossom. I needed to tell her to be careful of strangers—not to take carrots from creepy people.

"*Aehh* ..." Blossom called from above the granite outcropping.

I was more afraid for her than ever before.

Chapter 12

9/11

For many people, September 11, 2001, started as just another sunny fall day.

TUESDAY, 6:45 A.M.

Nothing went as planned.

China swung her head in a wide arc and slammed into the side of the alpaca birthing stall, grunting in panic, struggling to free herself from the partially born baby dangling beneath her tail. One of the baby's legs was twisted, stuck in the birth canal.

Its first breath came as a soft gasp.

The mother was long overdue. The day before, Pino left for an equestrian trade show in Wisconsin, kidding on the way to the airport about hanging a wide-load sign on the one-hundred-eighty-pound alpaca.

We researched problematic births in alpaca medical guides, bought a gallon of lubricant, rigged an oxygen tube splitter to enable two separate feeds from one tank, and set up a sleeping bag in the narrow center section between the stalls. I was prepared for the worst. I thought.

The simple pulley lead line I rigged through China's halter allowed some maneuverability while dealing with the needs of both ends—of both animals. I let it play out through my left hand, giving China a chance to relax and snugged an oxygen mask over the baby's face with my right.

It was the same smiley-face mask I had used on Blossom almost two years before. The mask's resemblance to Doctor Doolittle's fictional Pushmi-Pullyu character, with two heads at opposing ends of its body, brought a moment of respite and a smile.

China slumped down and started to roll.

"Don't roll!" With my free arm, I pushed hard on her rump and added pressure to the halter. She stopped and stared at me, surprised.

"I've got two legs and a head. Easy girl—You can do this— push!"

She was exhausted to the core and groaned in relief as the slippery bundle of life—a rather large bundle at that for an alpaca— was born into my arms.

Minutes later, I listened to the mama alpaca's soothing humming sounds as she tidied up, talked, and welcomed her little baby into the world.

8:50 A.M.

In retrospect, life seemed full of so much natural beauty that fine September day.

I carried the baby into the sun and laid her on a patch of thick grass, looked up into the crystal clear, azure sky and at China, nuzzling her newborn, coaxing it under her belly to nurse.

Blossom stood watching from the horse side of the paddock fence line.

"Blossom, come see the new baby." She didn't approach. The alpacas were interested in her, sometimes attempting to sniff and play, but eventually gave up. Once, Blossom tried, but—something about the alpaca's popcorn-like smell made her snort, roll, and squirm on the grass to rid herself of their odor.

Most times, Blossom stayed upwind.

9:00 A.M.

The phone in my back pocket rang. "Hello?"

"Mom, turn on the television. A plane just hit the World Trade Center! Where's Pino?" I heard the urgency in Glen's voice. "He's in Wisconsin at an industry trade show since yesterday. Was it a little plane?"

"Did you hear me?" He sounded frantic. "Get to the TV. Didn't Pino work there?"

Blossom followed me into the house, up the stairs, and circled down on the rug in front of the television. I sat on a large cushion beside her, my hand stiff, fidgety on her neck. My little fawn had grown into a sleek, beautiful doe, with a disposition to match.

But, then again, she had never been taught to hate.

Her head rested on my leg as I traced a path with my fingers around the velvety base of her ears, the softest part of her body.

"*Aehh* ..." She stretched her head toward mine.

How I wished to be able to lose myself in her innocence, unencumbered by the onslaught of anguish that surely would follow the day's events.

9:05 A.M.

An undulating blanket of thick black smoke wound its way toward the roof of the World Trade Center's North Tower in New York City. Unrelenting, as a serpent squeezing, tightening its coils into a solid mass of destruction, it engulfed one of the twin tower landmarks in lower Manhattan while a black-ringed fireball blasted another massive section of deadly debris on the people below.

It was rush hour.

Crews from every broadcast medium strained to maintain some professional decorum in the frantic aftermath of the catastrophe. Stunned eyewitnesses described seeing a commercial jetliner hit a skyscraper.

The phone lines were overloaded. At last, Pino got through. "We're watching on a huge screen they set up in the convention center. People here from New York are saying that it must be another terrorist bombing. Remember how paranoid my friends at the Port Authority were after the attack on the World Trade Center eight years ago? Whoever planned this wants that building full of people on a workday. Thousands of people could be there."

"Some newscasters are speculating this might be an accident. Could that be?"

"A commercial plane flying into a massive building in clear skies with no visibility problems? No way." Pino's voice sounded coarse, full of anger and disgust. "This is not an accident."

I stared at the television. "But, if it's a large jet, then where's its tail? I can't see anything sticking out of the building!" I gasped as another hunk of the towering structure blew out and fell away, and what appeared like confetti from a ticker-tape parade now filled the air. Papers, notes, documents, someone's doodles, pictures torn from thousands of frames, threads of consciousness, thrown to the winds. "Pino," I cried, "the people. How will they get out?"

We both knew the answer.

"I'll try to come home tomorrow. I can't reach my sons, and Flora works in one of the buildings at the WTC complex." Pino's son Michael was a New York police officer, and Flora, his wife, was pregnant with their first child. Pino's younger son Peter worked in midtown for a news network.

My mouth dropped in disbelief as a ball of fire blew through the middle of the second building, the South Tower. "Pino! I just saw it—another plane flew behind the building! Oh God, the people ..." I moaned in despair.

"Look, everybody here will be scrambling to get home. I'll try to get to Newark Airport. They'll probably close the tunnels and bridges. I'm sorry I'm not there with you. Don't worry. Stay safe. I love you." He started to say something else, but his voice caught, and he remained silent. That silence was all I needed to understand what he was feeling.

"I love you too. Don't worry; I'll be okay."

9:37 A.M.
The phone rang. I grabbed it. "Pino?"

"No. Hi, Anna. It's Ron from the Government Procurement Office. I thought I'd reach out to you early to get things started with our order. I'm on my way into the Pentagon. It's a gorgeous day. Listen, I need to know where you're shipping from."

"Hello. Ron? Turn on the news. A plane—"

"Aaaaaah! My God! No, No, NO!" he screamed before the phone connection died, followed by sustained abrasive crackling.

I never heard from him again.

It was too painful to find out why.

Television news anchor Katie Couric tried to keep her cool. "There has apparently been an explosion at the Pentagon."

A Pentagon Army officer said, "The air smells acrid, like the smell of a light bulb burning out." Frantic eyewitness accounts and camera footage revealed that another plane, the third plane, hit its target in the attack against America. All government buildings were on alert. The White House had been evacuated.

"The FAA has grounded all air traffic, nationwide," reported another broadcaster, Tom Brokaw. "This is an obvious terrorist attack."

10:28 A.M.

It must be an illusion. The building could not be leaning. Could it? Buildings didn't lean like that. I re-dialed Ron, then Pino, Glen, Mary, and my friends. All telephone circuits were jammed.

A deep red flame seethed within the North Tower, red and orange, like the cauldron of an erupting volcano. Blacker-than-black smoke spewed from a few floors below, swirling up, around, and into what must have been a sucking air source on the roof in a never-ending vertical rolling spin. Mesmerizing pyrodynamics, like an emotional safety valve, brought a brief moment of numbing peace.

Firefighters and rescue squads were everywhere. As witnesses to the chaos, they must have already known that this disaster had no fix. It was too big, too high, and too volatile. I saw their resilience turn into heartbreaking despair as they rotated into and out of what became known as "ground zero."

Breathless with anxiety, a newsman asked one firefighter, "Why are you going back in?" Confusion, sorrow, and soot were etched into the firefighter's face. He glanced into the world beyond the camera lens and said, "It's my job and,"—he swallowed, choking on his grief— "my brother may be in there."

In direct contrast with the anger and evil playing out on television, Blossom licked the tears from between my fingers when the twin towers collapsed into feathered plumes of debris and ash, and a great anvil-shaped yellow cloud crept through Lower

Manhattan—smothering—leaving all but the tallest spires in silhouette against the once perfectly blue sky—clear evidence of man's inhumanity to man.

I needed to get away and headed outside to the patio. Blossom took off, down the steps, toward the woods. The thrum of music, a bluegrass banjo, drifted up from the horse barn. I remembered that my friend Marge planned to ride Protto Call. I could see China's baby up and nursing, her long legs splayed for balance while China steadied its tiny rear end with her nose.

I waved to another dedicated jogger who lived nearby. Mary Ann waved back, as usual, but didn't stop to stretch and say hello to the alpacas, continuing her routine along the two-mile circuitous route.

Ten minutes later, I was back in front of the television.

10:40 A.M.

Could things get worse? Another report, a fourth plane, presumed hijacked, could be heading toward Washington, DC.

Not since the Cold War Fifties era, when our grade school desks served as protection from bombs, did I feel afraid or confused about the reasons why our country would be under attack.

It was always "over there" where bombs systematically targeted "the enemy." Is this what it's like to be at war? Would they just keep coming; plane after plane, bomb after bomb, like the London Blitz during WWII?

"It has now been confirmed by Somerset Airport that a United Airlines jet was hijacked and has gone down southeast of Pittsburg, Pennsylvania ...."

The world had changed too fast. I decided to watch the news for only a few minutes at a time, allowing only dribs and drabs of the catastrophe to siphon through. I walked down to the barn—surprised that birds continued to chirp, and the soft crunch of thick grass under my feet continued to please me.

News bulletins were blasting from the radio in the tack room. Marge, too, had been crying. We hugged.

"Have you seen Mary Ann?" she whispered, frightened. "You know that Andrew and his brother work at the World Trade Center, at Cantor Fitzgerald, the brokerage firm, right?"

Andrew was Mary Ann's husband. I choked up. "I can't imagine … I don't want to imagine …"

Marge's eyes shifted to the lone runner. "She's coming back." We opened the gates to meet her.

Marge bumped my hand. "Look at that."

Mary Ann was not alone. Her hand rested on Blossom's furry head and was licked in return. A soft smile, incongruous with the horror she was facing, offered a momentary respite.

The three of us reached out, held each other's hands, and hugged. My heart broke when I saw her bewilderment and again when she gave up wiping her tear-streaked face.

Her grief was palpable.

"Andrew hasn't called yet," she shivered the words through trembling lips. "He went in early today and—" She started to sob, and the tears flowed again.

"The phone lines are down; he needs time." I tried to sound hopeful. "Maybe he wasn't there."

We held on to each other for a long time.

What is it about running that soothes and helps people heal?

★ ★ ★

As the hours passed, I watched Mary Ann running, running, with a phone pressed to her head, trying to decipher what may have happened to her husband and brother-in-law and the collateral damage to her and their young daughters.

She was strong, but she was breaking—and so she ran.

Many people in Tewksbury were suffering. Loved ones and neighbors were lost, and people congregated on the historic streets, seeking peace and solace in an upside-down world too terrible to bear alone. Near the stream at the southern edge of Unicorn Hollow, a man I didn't know stopped to pet Blossom. She walked with him for a while and then came home. The next day, I met Jason and listened to his story about friends he had lost in the military. He called Blossom "the salve for my soul."

Animals have an innate sensitivity to emotional pain or injury. Who hasn't experienced an animal trying to comfort a hurt child? One of my fondest memories is of Justinian allowing a boy in a heavy wheelchair to bump to a stop against his leg. I expected him to jump away, but he didn't. What he did do, as naturally as if it were an everyday occurrence, was lower his head and nuzzle the youngster's hair. A caregiver told us it was the first time the child had tried to speak or reach out to touch in months.

★ ★ ★

Forty miles from where we stood the lights were snuffed out in the eyes of thousands of people in New York City. Hard to believe that life kept chugging along, albeit with a distinct limp.

Later, I filled in the blanks of my Alpaca Birthing Journal.

Date: September 11, 2001

Weight: 26 pounds

Name of China's baby: AMERICA

THE NATURE OF OUR LIGHT

Now in this wretched darkness,
Now when our country mourns its dead,
there is light. It shines
through our "ag on weary faces.
It leaps from torches searching
for the light of life.
It pours from the hearts of people
Giving lives in service to hope.

It radiates from the American soul
like Liberty's torch.
It is a beacon to the world; the sun
of our humanity, and gratitude
For life lived free.
It will remain an eternal flame
that never sleeps,
A path through this terrible night.

— *JEANNE HAMILTON TROAST 9/11/2001*

Chapter 13

Mistletoe and Holly

We moved slowly through Thanksgiving and Christmas in 2001. Pino's sons and their wives were safe, but generalized mourning enveloped so many, and each of us grasped for balance and stability wherever we could find it. As people gravitated to houses of worship looking for solace, I walked through the woods, poked my walking stick through snow, logs, and debris, en route to Blossom's hideaway.

Once there, within the tangle of brush and holly, I could detach myself from the worldwide turmoil and slip into sweet serenity. Her den was tight but cozy. Amazingly, it was gratitude for Blossom's friendship, honest and real, that helped bring the giggles back into my life.

A wispy wild rose vine snagged the pompom of my wool cap and yanked it from my head. My ears were freezing, but I couldn't help smiling—Mother Nature was still in charge of some things. Hat back on my head, ponytail tucked under, I whistled a tune not much worth remembering.

"Miss Blossom, you home?" I unbuckled my knapsack, put it and my stick down, and stooped to look inside the comfortable space under the holly tree—vacant, except for a few puffs of snow and a flattened mat of dry cushiony pine where she recently rested.

Off traipsing with the young piebald doe, I'll bet.

My gaze followed the natural lattice supporting framework, at the twigs broken in exactly the right places, and the ground padded with once glossy pine needles and aromatic cedar. No bad smells here. It was cold but comfortable. I sank down, cross-legged, and reached for my thermos of hot apple cider.

I needed a quiet place to think out the unexpected consequences from the latest newspaper article in the Hunterdon Observer.

Who would have anticipated the hit-or-miss idea I shared with a reporter could upstage a story featuring Governor Christie Todd Whitman? "Animal Lover Suggests Adopt-A-Deer Program," with a picture of Blossom and me, made the front page. Within days our mailbox was full of checks made payable to Adopt-A-Deer.

Now, what?

Some of the checks didn't even have return addresses. Yet, I would be my own worst enemy if I didn't continue to stand up for Blossom, and my values. Mom used to tell me to "pull yourself up by the bootstraps and go on."

I peeked outside at a world of grays, the sky as soft as the underbelly of a dove. My vantage from the hill allowed a view of Unicorn Hollow, beyond our house, and deep into the back pastures. The lights went on in the kitchen and front porch. Pino must have come up from the office. All seemed quiet on the farm, except for the blur of our mini-horses, Poncho and Sparky, as they chased each other through the snow—still, no sign of Blossom.

I thought about the unusual markings on the small piebald doe. We caught a glimpse of her, only once, as a fawn. Her face had splotches of white, beige, and brown fur, an oddity of sorts in a species with basic caramel coloring. A distinctive white patch of fur encircled her left eye and headed skyward to the tip of her ear. "Like an exclamation mark on a living patchwork quilt," I told Pino.

She reminded me so much of a little girl I once knew in the hospital. The wounds on the little girl's face had healed with patches of discoloration and keloids requiring plastic surgery but did nothing to detract from her lively spirit. She was resilient. As the old Chinese proverb says, "The weed that bends with the wind does not break."

★ ★ ★

New York, 1955

Sweet, gentle Viola. Right after her eighth birthday, she was well enough to leave the hospital.

The last injections of the day had been administered, the lights were dimmed, and the ward quieted. Viola stood on her mattress and waved to me from her bed in the next cubicle. She wore her pretty, new flannel pajamas with pictures of panda bears playing in front of gigantic yellow ice cream cone clouds. She pointed to the book in her hand and beckoned me to join her.

Not Daniel Boone again.

I nodded. Of course, we all knew Viola would be leaving with her new adoptive parents soon. Yesterday, Mom brought the scarf I had been given for Christmas. I wanted Viola to have it.

She lifted her blanket for me to get under the covers. "I'm scared," Viola said, snuggling up.

"Yeah? But you're looking at it the wrong way. Just flip it around. The other side of scared is excitement, happiness, and fun. All the kids think you're lucky."

"I really like Mr. and Mrs. Bradlee." Viola's enthusiasm for her new family was catchy. She needed to talk, but it would only happen in her own time, in her way.

I'd almost finished reading her another chapter of Daniel Boone when she pushed the picture book down on my stomach.

"What?" I considered my small friend, now squeezed to the edge of her bed to make more room for me. Deep whitish pink splotches remained on her face, like the discoloration of a flower petal as it starts to wither. A year ago, she had fallen into hot tar, and she habitually tried to hide the burned side of her head, as if she were ashamed.

She whispered, more to herself than to me. "You said ... I'm, ah ... pretty, right?"

"Right. Very pretty."

"But"—she raised her hand to the melted part of her skin—"my face looks like I rubbed too hard and washed all the brown color out ... they want me to call them Mommy and Daddy." Her thoughts drifted, and her eyes filled with bewildered sadness.

Cuddled close, comfortably resting her chin on my shoulder, and holding one side of the book while I held the other, I said, "You ready? All together now." We recited the poem in unison. "Daniel Boone, at twenty-one, came with his tomahawk, knife, and gun ... home from the French and the Indian Wars, to North Carolina and the Yadkin Shore—"

"How come his raccoon hat got a tail on it?" Viola interrupted. "I don't understand—maybe to keep flies off his neck?"

I thought about it. "That makes sense. Maybe there's lots of bugs on the Yadkin Shore in North Carolina."

"Keep reading." She turned the page. "Do you think they'll make a good family?" She made a face with a funny twist, but I knew she was serious.

"You kidding me? They already love you, we all see it. Besides, just look at your new doll and pretty clothes. They're even more excited than you are—about YOU!" I tickled her until she scrunched her body in giggles.

"I think they have a yard. And, we're gonna go get a puppy! I get to choose!" Her dark hazel eyes filled her face, a tweak of sadness pulling at the corners.

"Wow, are you lucky! So, why the sourpuss face?" I gave her a playful nudge.

"Uh ... I'm gonna miss you. You're my family too." She started to cry. I reached up to fool with the ringlets on her head.

"Yeah, me too. You'll always be with me in my heart, don't you know?" We stayed quiet for a long time. The reading had served its purpose.

"Annie, thanks for the beautiful scarf." She cupped my hand in hers and kissed my fingers, one at a time.

"Sweet dreams. I love you too."

Deep in thought, I climbed down and watched the bunny ears on my slippers jiggle as I moped off to my bed in the next cubicle.

Not fair. She was learning, if you were damaged, there would be times when the need to hide would sting.

I thought of how furious I looked in Mom's favorite picture of the trip we took to Jones Beach that year. It was simple to figure out why. If you really knew me. Mama held our hands and smiled at the camera. Mary struck a funny pose while I squirmed and twisted, trying to break out of my mother's grip. I kicked out and begged her to let me get away from the imminent picture.

"No, no, NO!" I remember pleading. Some people on the beach turned to look. Why wouldn't Mama let me go? Why didn't my father listen to me and put the camera down? That morning, he'd made it clear that I was nothing but trouble for him. My arm ached where he had grabbed me.

Couldn't they see I wasn't wearing the tee shirt that covered my burns? I still have the picture. It makes me sad.

Isn't it curious how some memories cannot be glazed over, even by time?

★ ★ ★

The crunch of footsteps interrupted my memory. Pino's face popped into the entrance of Blossom's den, showing the wear and tear of a strenuous trade show season for our company, and the overall trauma of the past few months. His broad smile was like sunshine to me.

"Thought you might be up here. Can I join the party?" He crawled in and sat with his back against the trunk of the holly. He pulled a paper from his pocket. "An e-mail from Friends of Deer. Remember Pat, from the march in Princeton? She read about your Adopt-A-Deer plan in the Observer. More checks in the mail today."

"Oh, no."

"Come on; it could be a positive thing."

"I doubt it." I took the letter. "But, every piece of publicity incites angry phone calls. They scare me. The police take notes but don't do anything."

Dear Anna,

Just want to comment on the excellent article written by Lilly Dorshak. The picture of you with Blossom is so wonderful! Your story takes a different path than much that has been written about deer. Personally, I think your approach will be the most effective yet in the humane approach of managing deer. Deer can and should be enjoyed, and you certainly got that across.

In the past few years, deer have been vilified by the press to the point where the public has been spoon-fed by the media to regard them as "vermin." The picture of you and Blossom is proof-positive that deer can be as affectionate as domesticated animals. If we can get across to the public just how smart they are, they may rise to the respect status of whales, dolphins, and elephants. They certainly do deserve it.

Hopefully, the Observer article is the starting point of media attention that will attract a wider audience. Your local celebrity status should also have a positive impact on your town deer activities.

It is a pleasure knowing you.

Pat Scala

Friends of Deer

"Hope she's right," I said.

"Still no response from the wildlife biologist in Canada," Pino said. "What's his name? I get the feeling he doesn't want to be drawn into the controversy here. When did you send him the pictures of Blossom?"

"Mark Fraker. Two weeks ago." He nodded. "He doesn't realize how special Blossom is. He may think we're radical-type activists—just trouble. Give it more time, then you might—"

"*Aehh* ..." Big, bold, and beautiful Blossom blocked the entrance. We moved to give her space.

It got crowded, fast.

"Too cold for smooching." Pino wiped his face on his scarf, but Blossom's kisses kept coming.

I pulled a tissue from my jacket—laughing so hard, I cried.

We looked at each other, realizing, for the time being, the fairy tale was still true.

Chapter 14

Hiding in Plain Sight

The cold air smelled earthy and held the subtle smokiness from a far off fire.

Sitting cross-legged in the entrance of Blossom's den, with a clear line-of-sight to our home, it was apparent why she showed up at odd hours to welcome us, even before we unlocked the door.

A shaft of late day sun created misty art forms out of my swirling breath. My gaze drifted to Blossom, cozily curled behind me, realizing that life with her would always be an adventure.

I fussed over minor housekeeping—or "den-keeping"—jobs that satisfied my psyche, most likely the result of some latent nesting syndrome, or perhaps the article on enhancing energy vibes through Chinese "Feng Shui" design I'd read. I fluffed pine cushioning, discarding all but the cleanest leaves, tucked a vine into the wall.

I had packed a thermos of cider, an apple, a blow-up cushion and, the piece de resistance, a new ball of mistletoe dangling from a loop of bright red satin ribbon. The perfect spot to hang it was just inside the entrance where a vine interlocked its way through a thick leafy-green branch. I fussed with it until it felt right.

Okay, better. Pleased with myself, I hummed a tune as sunlight filtered haphazardly through the twiggy roof. My eyes flicked over each surface with a loving glance.

My thermos of apple cider was still hot, perfect for sipping on cold days like this. While Blossom munched carrots, I got the chance to inflate the blow-up pillow I found in Pino's old camping duffle bag. My handiwork completed, I sat down, the pillow belched, Blossom scrambled, and my butt sank to the ground.

"Oops!" The big bang.

"Lookee, lookee here, nothing to be afraid of," I babytalked, held up the fattened tube. Blossom hesitated, but trusted me, and circled down near my crossed legs. I brushed the smooth hair under her rainbow collar.

"You smell like new meadow grass."

In the distance, a diesel pickup accelerated, then slowed and wound its way to the ridge above the granite outcropping behind us. The Conklin's land included the woods buffeting Wildwood Road to the north. Their driveway circled that way.

I was not comfortable with living on constant alert, like walking on eggshells, waiting to outmaneuver a predator, as a deer would. Over the years, my conception of what was real, and what I naively wished for, took a one-hundred-eighty-degree turn. Now, when I gazed into Blossom's inquisitive dark eyes, I began to consider our lovely town from another perspective. As an invisible cage of rules, a crucible with too many licenses to kill in too many uncaring hands.

"Blossom, if I could—if there were a place, a safe place to go—I would take you away."

Blossom's head jerked up, on heightened alert. She stared through the foliage, ears swiveling—one forward, the other back. My eyes shut involuntarily. I strained to filter the distinct sounds of voices from background noises: a snapping twig, dried leaves crackling, brushed to the side by movement. They stopped. I waited. Steady footfalls now, closer but quieter, slow and measured.

A barely audible voice droned like an eerie lullaby carried by an unexpected breeze.

"Blossom ... where are you?"

I never fathomed that the saying "my blood ran cold" had anything to do with actual biology. Wrong. A distinct chill ran up my spine, and I froze, paralyzed by indecision.

Except for the hair rising slowly along Blossom's neck and back, she remained dead quiet. Her intense eyes communicated a signal as direct as a stop sign.

Don't move!

Trust her. She knows.

I strained to listen—

Another voice called, "Blossom," and now, distinct snaps—shuffling sounds of someone walking, closing the distance. Too far away to determine his path. *Please let Pino see them from the house.*

One of the men said, "They say she'll show up if you call her by name. She likes people." He seemed to chuckle, cleared his throat. In a sickening falsetto, attempting to sound friendly, he called, "B l o s s o m, come out, come out, wherever you are. Let's have a good look at you ..."

It must feel like this in war, hiding in a bunker, waiting for the whistling to stop—for a bomb to explode.

I lowered my head and rested my hand on her hip. Touched her so she would realize she was not alone—that I was not alone. I tried to concentrate on Blossom's foot pressing hard against my boot.

The sunlight flicked off, then on, like an electric light switch. It was inevitable. We were hiding in plain sight. They would find us.

Breathe slow—five counts in, six counts out.

I heard the unmistakable metal-on-metal clicks of a gun.

Who doesn't know that sound? I froze.

Cowering, I stared at the ball of mistletoe hanging from its red ribbon near the entrance. Red. The most outlandish, out-of-place color in the winter woods. Reaching over Blossom, I eased the ribbon off its twig, horrified when the loop of satin slipped between my gloved fingers, and the ornament plopped on Blossom's belly, then rolled to the ground. She stared at me wide-eyed and moved her head in a quick, disgusted-like shake.

"Did you hear something?" The person below us spoke in a hushed voice. He was coming closer.

"Be quiet, listen," the other one said.

The edges of panic closed in. I considered running out, flailing and screaming like a wounded bird, making myself a decoy so Blossom could run away. Then I recalled a story of a woman shot while waving her gloved hands to chase away hunters. The defense attorney excused the shooting based on her white gloves being mistaken for the white tails of fleeing deer.

Blossom's nostrils flared. She did not move, so neither did I. "Get off my property!" I jumped at the booming voice of our neighbor, David, shouting from the ridge.

"Shit. Shit. Shit," the person nearest us hissed, cursed, and, from the sounds I recognized, must have fallen in a deep pile of debris and decaying wood, where dead leaves and bark turned black, soggy, and didn't crunch anymore.

"There are no trespassing signs all over these woods," Pino yelled from below.

The man started to run and tripped again.

Pino passed by us, gesturing downward with his hand, his voice an urgent whisper. "Stay put!

"The safety better be on your rifle," he shouted. "You should know better. You'll kill somebody, hunting near houses.

You from around here?" He sounded restrained. "What's your name?"

I shuddered. *He saw the gun*!

"Yeah, okay, we're going. Didn't see 'no hunting' signs posted. Anyway, we only wanted a look at that deer." His voice changed to a whine.

"Shut up!" his friend bellowed. "You don't have to say anything. We have rights!"

Pino was furious. "You're trespassing on private land. I watched you and your buddy scout the hillside. You passed at least two 'no hunting' signs within the last few minutes. Get your story straight."

"Like I just told you, we wanted to take a look at the deer they talk about in the papers. We're outta here."

"Looking? With a gun?" Pino wouldn't let up.

"Leave me alone." The rustle of dried debris grew fainter as they climbed toward the pickup.

David and the other hunter were arguing loudly. David was a large man, but not a young man. Our mild-mannered scientist neighbor aggressively defended his right to keep people off his property while protecting Blossom at the same time. "You have some nerve. Never step foot on my property again! I have your license plate number."

"Go, David!" I rolled to my hands and knees, prepared to crawl outside, but Blossom blocked my exit with her body. I moved to go by her, and she blocked me again. I decided to wait.

A few minutes passed before she took a tentative step outside, all her senses probing. It was another full minute before I crawled out of our hideout, turned, and peered over the roof like a meerkat on sentry duty. The trespassers had loaded their weapons into the cab of their pickup. Finally, they left.

"Blossom, you okay girl?" I bent to kiss her and noticed my trembling hands. "What if—?"

She yawned and did one of her full-body stretches and head-to-tail shakes, bumped my hand, and positioned herself for a back scratch. "*Aehh* …" as if to say, glad that's over. She walked away into the woods.

I called after her. "That's it? No hug to celebrate our escape? Nothing else?"

She should be the poster child for the survival of the fittest.

Deer are flight animals; speed is their best defense. She could have run away.

A few weeks before, she had defended me against a buck double her size, who came too close to us in the paddock. She lowered herself, crept forward, charged, and reared. With a relentless succession of fast blows, she pounded him with her powerful front legs until he turned away. He never fought back, only backed away, surprised at the onslaught. I couldn't tell if she was guarding me or was merely possessive.

"You would be one heck of a date," I remembered saying. "The buck seemed nice."

★ ★ ★

"This has to stop!" Pino said. "It's absurd! Your life was in jeopardy because she's become a prize."

"I know … it was terrifying."

"I can imagine," he said. "When I saw those men paralleling the hill, I called David. He saw the pickup parked in the trees and had his boots on. He figured they were after Blossom. He was scared to death when I told you you were in there with her."

"So, what's next, the police again?" I asked. I pressed the ache in my temples. "As they say, 'If a bad guy has a gun'—and if the good guys have guns ... then what? A shootout at the OK Corral? With stupid logic, someone likely gets killed."

I replayed the terror for him and wept, blubbering between the words, "I'm ... I'm afraid. They want to snuff her out because she's 'somebody,' and they're not. Just for a trophy? She just wants to make friends. Who's going to protect her if we don't?" I sobbed and let the tears flow.

"*Shhh* ..." He smoothed the hair back from my face and held me. "Blossom never left you to 'make friends' with those guys. She knows who her friends are."

Chapter 15

Renfru

L ooking back on the way he risked showing himself, I should have realized who he was.

"Wow," I whispered, captivated by the buck's graceful majesty. His symmetrical antlers reached into the blue, white-tufted sky, each point a testament to his strength and age. His tawny and chestnut coat gleamed in the sunlight, muscles rippling beneath in a blend of power and elegance. Each step was a display of poise and nobility, his dark eyes reflecting the ancient wisdom of the forest.

Despite the warm sun, the air was crisp. He stayed near the base of the patio boulders, at times scratching his neck against a poplar, and nibbling bits of grass—but mainly watching the three of us.

There was no snorting or foot-stomping demands for Blossom's attention and submission. Instead, he lowered his head in a more subdued, gracious signal of friendliness.

"Such tenderness ... Pino, notice how soft his eyes are when he looks at her."

Blossom took her time, finally rising into a lackadaisical stretch. Without taking her eyes off the buck, she nonchalantly crunched the end of a carrot I offered. Then as if pretending she hadn't noticed his attention, she sashayed down the stone steps, pausing on each one to glance here and there—teasing him.

"If she could giggle, she'd be giggling," Pino said. "What a little flirt," I said.

The buck's barrel-chest heaved a response, somewhere between a cough and a sigh. He looked relieved and bowed over his leg.

"He doesn't appear overly concerned with our presence. Reminds me of the yearling we fed through the winter a few years ago," Pino said.

I studied the buck, noticed the bulbous deformity on his right front foot. "Look at his ankle."

"It's Renfru. The one who limped to the house every night for horse chow, remember?" Pino stepped closer. "Remember me?"

Nose up, the buck snorted—in a nice way. His ears twitched a bit, but that was all.

"He's not afraid," Pino said.

"What's wrong with this picture? I mean, what happened to the typical macho thing about males fighting to seduce, conquer, and breed, like on documentary television?"

"Just about sex?" Pino said. "Nope, not this time. He's obviously romancing her."

Renfru approached Blossom with the decorum of an aristocrat, frequently stopping and waiting as if looking for her approval. He appeared polite, almost shy.

"Oh," I sighed. "He's wonderful."

"She's seducing him, not the other way around," Pino said softly. "I see the signs."

Blossom eased closer, brushed her nose against his, allowed him to lift her collar to her ears, before letting it slip back. The scene was a visual gift, too precious to miss.

I whispered. "Like Gone with the Wind. You know, the part where she—"

"*Shush.*"

Blossom circled his body and stood squarely next to him, side by side, their faces touching intermittently. They stayed, breathing each other's breath, her lungs filling as he exhaled, back and forth between them.

"I choose you," his actions seemed to say. Blossom touched her nose to his shoulder and then turned and came back up the steps to us.

"What is it, Blossom?" I straightened her collar.

A mellow "*aehh ...*" followed by a lick on my hand was her answer. She pulled the rest of her carrot off the table and ate it, then turned back.

"Well, how about that?" Pino laughed.

"Excuse me, but did she just ask permission to go off with him?"

Without any aggressive behavior, Renfru coaxed Blossom to walk with him, into the woods.

"Do you suppose that other animals are capable of this type of interaction? Dogs and cats play together, but what we just saw takes it to another level of sensitivity and love, don't you think?"

"I can't believe they allowed us to watch," Pino said.

From somewhere below a wind chime echoed in a whisper of wind. I swung Pino's hand. "Ah, the bells are ringing, there's stardust in the air. Tra-la, tra-la, it must be love."

"She reminds me of you." He raised a single eyebrow in that seductive gesture that always made me laugh. "Dance?" He held out his arms to me.

I smiled at the invitation. The music was there, but only we heard it.

★ ★ ★

Three days later, and still no sign of Blossom. I tried to convince myself that Nature was in charge of things. It was natural. Besides, she's savvy, and Renfru survived longer than most deer in our area.

I was on my way to pick up the mail when the boxy little mail truck stopped at our corner. Don, the postman, waved, reached into his pocket, and brought out an apple. "Is Blossom around?" He handed me a bundle of mail secured by rubber bands and placed the apple on top.

"Thanks." I shrugged to hide my anxiety. "She met a fella, of course."

"Really? Go figure ... kids."

I glanced at the Canadian return address on the large manila envelope. "I've been waiting for this. If you see her, drop me a note, okay Don?"

"Sure thing." He saluted. "We're prayin' for her."

I waited for him to drive away before hurrying to the office.

I cleared an area on my desk and removed a small book, letter and a binder of documents from the bulky envelope. "Pino, look what the postman brought for guess who?" I tossed him the apple. "And, here's the package from Mark." I scanned the note. "He's planning a trip to Washington, DC in a few months—he thinks Blossom could bring awareness to his project for humane wildlife control. Says her personality could touch a few hearts.

"Listen to this." I brought the book to his desk. *A Rescue That Moved the World*, by Mark Fraker. I read aloud:

"Point Barrow, Alaska, 1988. Two California gray whales made a run for freedom early Wednesday evening, leaving behind a series of breathing holes cut through the ice by Eskimos with chainsaws and popping up moments later in a channel in the ice cut by a Soviet icebreaker."

A *Los Angeles Times* article was folded neatly under the cover, which I also read aloud. "They seem to sense something is happening,' Mark A. Fraker, a senior environmental scientist with Standard Oil of Alaska, said earlier in the day.

"'I am gratified that the California gray whales have been released to the open sea,' Reagan said in a statement read by a White House spokesman. 'The human persistence and determination by so many individuals on behalf of these whales shows mankind's concern for the environment.'"

I flipped through documents, feasibility deer and black bear studies, copies of letters from The Smithsonian Zoo endorsing research for an elephant vaccine, the Wild Horse Sanctuary in California in support of testing an equine vaccine. Wherever the need existed to humanely control wildlife populations, the new vaccine called SpayVac promised a viable answer.

Too excited to sit still, I grabbed Pino's hand. "This is the answer. The timing is perfect. Like with dogs and cats, the deer population can be managed humanely. Fewer killings, less agony."

"Blossom will be safer."

"It sounds too good to be so easy," Pino's voice faltered. "Going against the gun lobby's agenda can never be easy."

Chapter 16

Uninvited Caller

Days became humdrum, less vibrant, like a bottle of bubbly champagne gone flat. Patiently, we waited for Blossom to come home. I divided the time between our business, the comforting routine of caring for the farm, and riding sure-footed Simba into the steeper wooded areas where I wouldn't venture on my own.

We hurried through breakfast. Pino had a full day of business meetings, and rain was forecast to slow traffic into New York City.

"Blossom is a free spirit. It's her first sleep-away," he kidded, brushing a few toasted crumbs from his tie.

"Don't laugh. I know."

He shook his head. "I don't believe it. We're suffering from empty nest syndrome after only a week. Cheer up. Renfru is a good guy."

I put my arms around him and kissed him goodbye. "Be careful on the roads."

The wind picked up steadily over the next few hours. Before the drizzle turned into a downpour, I raced to the barns to feed the horses and alpacas, stopping from time to time to concentrate on Blossom—willing her to hear my thoughts. I sensed she knew exactly where I was.

The gray day turned dark by the time I walked into the kitchen and turned on the lights. Pint-sized Kaya hated the rain and headed for the safety of her hooded bed in the kitchen. Caruso was deep into a cup of sunflower seeds.

Time to relax.

The preparations for dinner were complete. I poured wine into the delicate crystal glass Mary had given me and held it up to the light to admire the intricate, hand-painted blue lilacs spiraling into its slender, pewter base. She'd written on the card, "Don't break it."

Glen would be calling from Hawaii. I could almost hear my son's animated conversation about his new venture. "Mom, so many people need addiction counseling, and I'm good at it. The way I look at counseling is new and unique. We'll talk later."

At 7 p.m., the phone rang.

Spread-eagle on top of his cage, Caruso, all green, yellow, puffed, and feathery, went into his routine. "Allo, wanna go to the opera? *La la la la la la laaa ...*"

Cramming the receiver between my head and shoulder, I said, "Hey, Glen."

Someone coughed.

"Glen? Yoo-hoo. You there?"

There was a silence, and then the breathy, stilted voice and more wheezing.

"Ah ... what are we having for supper, Anna?" Prickles of fear raised the hairs on my neck.

"Anna ... are you listening?" His tone became annoyed. "I'm speaking to you, Anna."

My next words surprised even me. "You'll need an inhalant before that condition gets worse." I sounded lame. Too late to take them back.

He didn't answer. Somewhere, a car door slammed. "Who are you?"

"Nice. We have wine tonight, Anna."

How does he know? Oh, God. He can see me!

I squinted and peered through the dark window. My reflection bounced back at me like a two-way mirror. Gripping the handle of a knife, I stepped back and groped for the bank of light switches near the refrigerator, pushing them down.

The darkness was as absolute as a nightmare. I strained to adjust my eyes.

"Too bad about Blossom," he said.

Don't ask what he means.

Keep your enemies talking, and in front of you, someone once told me. The silence became awkward. He sounded dead serious—his tone, pattern of speech, the long pauses. The way he repeated my name, even how he struggled to breathe, repulsed me.

"Blossom's mine now," he said.

His words struck like a punch. *She's his?*

"What are you so angry at?" I asked. "What happened to make you like this?"

"I've had enough of you," he growled. "She's mine!"

"Go to hell!"

I slammed the phone into its cradle.

Damn him!

I had forgotten about the knife clutched in my hand until its tip poked my leg. The thought of stabbing something living, of slicing through flesh in anger, disgusted me. I shoved it across the counter and heard it clatter against the wall.

The steady rumble of rain muted all sound. Tiny LED lights on various appliances helped me navigate through the darkened house. With arms outstretched, I shuffled into the den.

What did he mean by "too bad about Blossom"?

Caruso flapped his wings against his cage, startling me.

I'll get Caruso! Perched on my arm like a predatory hawk, he'll attack, wings flapping furiously, screaming with a piercing cry. Talons extended and beak ready to snap, he'll tear into the unsuspecting intruder with relentless ferocity. Always holding on.

Though, admittedly, a knife made more sense.

Pino would be home soon. All the windows and doors were shut, but not every door was locked.

Go easy; take your time.

I dialed the police. The officer listened while I told him of the threatening call from a man asking me, by name, what was on the menu, and oh-by-the-way, "it was nice that we had wine with dinner." I sounded ridiculous.

Anger blurred my vision.

Check everything—stay alert. Next, I punched in Pino's cell number.

There was a thump at the door.

What was that?

I crouched below the windows.

The door opened, Caruso shrieked, and the overhead lights glared.

"*Aaahhh!*" I screamed.

"What's wrong? Why is the house dark?" Pino called out.

I ran to him. "He was watching me, I'm sure of it," I blurted out.

An angry flush spread from Pino's neck to his cheeks, then to his forehead. He picked up the flashlight, took my heavy walking stick from behind the door, and headed outside. "The ground is soft. Anyone standing near the house would have left footprints. If he's still around, I'll find him!"

Later, over reheated butternut squash soup, I talked about how delusional and disconnected the caller sounded.

"Didn't you tell the police he was watching you?"

"Of course. But, when the officer asked me if I was positive, what could I say? Only that the guy knew I was cooking and having a glass of wine?"

The phone rang. Reluctantly, I lifted the receiver and listened, uncertain if I should say anything.

"Allo, wanna go to the opera with Caruso? *La, la* ..."

"Caruso," Glen said, "put Mom on the phone. "Mom?" he repeated. "Earth to Mom ..."

I breathed a sigh of relief, "Glen ..." but the gut-level outrage of our vulnerability was becoming more evident.

This wouldn't be the last time.

Chapter 17

A Friend in Need

That fall's pattern of storms tormented the Northeast, uprooting trees and turning the ground into a muddy trap that could suck the boots right off your feet. Being careful didn't have much to do with it.

"*She's mine*," played nonstop in my mind.

A break in the weather provided the opportunity. No more waiting, moping around, hoping for a tap from Blossom's foot at the patio door, her *aehh* call through an open window or, better yet, a game of hide-and-seek near the barn.

I adjusted the binocular strap around my neck, pulled my warm shearling hat from the closet, and shoved my feet into rubber boots. Pino's yellow leather gloves were way too big, but my phone fit conveniently into a flexible pouch sewed on the back, so I grabbed them.

As I started my climb, Nancy and a few dedicated joggers, turned onto Wildwood. They slowed, and she waved a pink-gloved hand at the hill.

"Seriously?" she shouted. "Tell me you're not going up there—it's been devastated." She frowned. "Be careful of copperheads, especially around those boulders. Sleeping or awake, they freak me out."

"Thanks for the bulletin." The thought of inhabiting the same space as a hibernating snake sent shivers down my spine—*eek*!

"Still no sign of Blossom?" She continued to jog in place. "I'll keep my eyes open. Gotta catch up with the girls."

I continued to the granite outcropping three-quarters of the way up the hill.

So much had changed. The storms had taken their toll.

In the now macabre setting, the air was thick with the aromas of damp earth and musky split wood. A once-grand oak had shattered several feet off the ground, its heartwood forever splayed open, like the pages of a book. Branches pierced the ground everywhere.

The holly tree had survived, but a stray limb had crushed the roof of Blossom's den, its network of vines now shuddering like some twiggy ornamental fringe. Images of her trapped inside forced a grief-stricken wail.

"Blossom!"

I yanked at the crisscrossed branches. Wood cracked, vines parted until there was an opening wide enough for me to squeeze through. I peered into the shadows where I knew she would blend, shoved debris aside, probing for anything—blood, hair, her breakaway collar.

Nothing.

A dingy red satin ribbon and a ball of once-live mistletoe hung on a twig. I touched it, smiled and made it swing with a flick, but left it there for luck. My jeans were saturated; it didn't matter. Kneeling on the little patch of ground comforted me. My place too.

Now what?

Eventually, I backed out of the space. A thorny vine yanked off my hat—like old times. I laughed— "I'm coming back with my clippers," I threatened.

The hope in my heart and determination in my step made it particularly dangerous for me to be trudging up the mud-slicked hill. Almost immediately, I slipped and fell to one knee, a stern warning to slow down. I pulled a bag of oatmeal cookies from my inside pocket and sacrificed one in Blossom's name.

Careful to avoid wet patches of mosses and lichen covering the rock, I climbed to the first flat level for a better view. I hurriedly brought out my binoculars. Fidgeting with the dials distorted every tree into a mishmash of disorienting shapes. One eyepiece at a time, I learned to adjust the focus.

I remember thinking that mastering the art of bird watching requires patience and focusing skills—without becoming queasy. The higher vantage point provided a new perspective over the tops of mid-canopy trees, stone walls, hedges, and the cypress wind barricade our neighbor, George, planted half a century ago.

I refocused on his very pink house tucked behind a stand of craggy pines. George called it Rose Cottage.

No Blossom, No Renfru. No deer.

I squinted through my binoculars for a better view up to the next level. Flakes of blue-gray lichen clung like peeling paint on much of the rock, but the climb appeared more accessible, with notched-out areas for easy grab and toeholds. I ate another of Blossom's cookies and decided to go for it.

The sound of a car on our gravel drive broke my concentration. I zoomed in on the threatening shape of a hooded man stepping from the driver's side, fists jammed in the pockets of his jacket, bent forward as if walking against a stiff wind. He appeared to be measuring or scouting the premises.

To avoid detection, I crouched low until his car pulled away. I needed to get home. With a sense of urgency, I began my descent, retracing my steps as fast as I dared.

Too fast!

I slipped on a clump of lichen. Arms windmilling, clawing for a handhold, I slid toward the edge. In slow-motion, I watched my right leg and boot above me, heard the sizzle of my jacket ripping, the grind of solid rock against my binoculars, and the final jerk of the strap on my neck when it broke free.

For a second, I thought it was a good thing to land in the mud. Or so I hoped, until odd splitting noises from rain-weakened vegetation turned into underground grunts and slurps, the ground shimmied away from its rocky substrate, and all hell broke loose.

Suddenly, a jumbled mass of wood tugged my boot and sock off, while the mudflow surged over and under my body. A blur of yellow floated by—then disappeared.

My phone!

Sliding, like skiing, allowed me the chance to maneuver. I grasped bare-handed for branches, roots, anything—forcing myself to relax, I struggled to protect my head.

My vision blurred, yet the glint of color looked real. And, the deer—there was a deer, I thought—bounding toward me, cutting closer as I dropped—with an underbelly as white as fresh snow. That looked real too.

I crashed broadside into a hedgerow of overgrown bushes, cushy with years of leafy buildup within its woody stalks.

Little attempts at movement—toes, fingers, neck—assured no numbness or broken parts. I could make a fist, first with my right hand, then with my left. Except for the throb in my lower back, I lay comfortably on the pillow of spongy debris, exhausted.

Something moved across my foot.

No, no! Something crawling on my ankle? A snake?

My eyes and mouth tight—shut in fear—I sucked a sharp breath through my nose and remained still.

A breath of air whooshed over my face, followed by a bump to my head, and long pulls from a warm tongue starting to clean up the mess on my face.

"*Aehh …*"

"Blossom!" I blinked away enough crud to look into the gentle eyes and furry face of my sweet friend. She licked a path from my ears to my nose, then across my forehead.

The sound of molars grinding dirt was awful. She spit it out, yawning noisily, as usually happened when she swallowed too much air while grooming extra dirty animals. Like me.

"Wait." I rolled over my arm.

Without thinking, I gripped her ankle—the curve of her back leg—her tail. It must have hurt.

"*Aehh …*"

She shifted to support my weight and allowed me to crawl, inch by inch, until I could rest on her back—and yet, she didn't move, not even a foot—only turning to nuzzle my neck. We stayed that way, with my face and hands buried in her dense fur, until I regained stability.

For many minutes nature showed extraordinary patience, and time stood still. A single tear fell from my eye—in awe of this incredible animal. "Thank you, my girl."

She was tall enough for me to lean on as we headed home. Each step made the next one more manageable, but I cannot remember who was pulling, who was pushing. We were partners. My head was pounding by the time we reached the front door.

"*Aehh …*" Blossom headed for the bowl of sweet cherries in the kitchen. I took two anti-inflammatory pills and grabbed an ice pack from the freezer. I needed to call the police.

"Please, don't stay away so long."

As I watched her weave her way to the ridgeline, the obvious answer to the wonder of Blossom was also the truest one. She was there for me.

As I read this years later, I am forced, with a shrug, to admit the improbable image of a deer, even so large a doe as Blossom, carrying, even walking, a person down a hill. I will say only this:

There comes a time in life when a friendship is stamped into eternity. This was such a time.

It will always seem like yesterday to me.

THE PROMISE

I will comfort you. Hold me close in your heart.
My tears are sacred, my compassion deep.
I carry knowledge of the deepest part of you.
You and I are survivors, embracing
Life as it is, aware
Joy is a choice.

I am the one you turn to in suffering.
Together we give birth to new ideas;
New ways of thinking.
I ride the currents of your life
Teaching you to be grateful for all
You have and all you will become.

I am the companion you give your self
In one tremendous act of love.
I am witness to your spirit, the verification
Of your giving soul. In the stillness
I am your peace.

— JEANNE HAMILTON TROAST

Chapter 18

A Lie Worth Considering

I wanted to skip along the snow-covered path and kick up my heels. Christmas is Christmas, right?

Instead, perhaps as a nod to convention, Pino and I locked arms and satisfied ourselves with listening to our boots crunch past snowcapped fenceposts along the way to the veranda of a sprawling home.

"Listen ..." he said. We paused as the last notes from a rich baritone sang Ave Maria. The scent of burning logs, the subdued clink of dishes, the chatter of guests, and bubbles of laughter filled the air. The local Tewksbury Trail riding club holiday party was in full swing.

"Jeff calls this his cottage." Pino smiled, looking up at the 25-foot ceiling beams.

Vivian, Jeff's wife, was cooking when we joined the crowd in the kitchen. "Pino, Anna!" She lifted a spoon in greeting. "Merry Christmas. How's your deer? She's famous now. Come, have something to eat. Get some wine."

Towering centerpieces of fresh vegetables and fruits circled with artichoke-shaped candles, wicker baskets of rolls, and an enormous variety of foods filled a long buffet table against one wall. Pino angled our box of pastries between a bowl of chocolate-covered strawberries and a platter of cookies.

I slipped out of my coat and spotted my friend Ellie gesturing for me to wait. I blew her a kiss. "Be right back. One minute."

Ellie called over the din. "Heads up! There's an elk in the closet."

"They invited an elk?" I laughed, waved happily at friends decked out in their holiday best, and continued into the two-story foyer.

I should have heeded her advice, at least listened more carefully! Coat in hand, I opened the door. The overhead light switched on. From beneath hanging coats, the stu!ed head of a massive elk poked out.

"*Aaah!*" Instinctively, I backed away from the nothingness behind its glass eyes.

People close by noticed. Jeff hurried over and took my coat. "I apologize. The taxidermist delivered it a few hours ago." He pushed the door shut. Come with me. There's somebody I want you to meet."

"Just like taking a shower at the Bates Motel." I grinned, not entirely in amusement. "I'm never going to look into a closet the same way again."

"You wouldn't listen," Ellie whispered, tugging at my sleeve. "White or red? I'll go for the wine."

"Red."

Walls decorated with big game hunting trophies and paintings of wildlife created a woodsy, lodge-like atmosphere, and firelight shadow-boxed with a stag head mounted above the hearth. Partygoers gathered around the piano, singing, if they knew the words, humming the rest. It didn't matter.

A distinguished man in a brown tweed jacket unfolded himself from an oversized wing chair and approached. Jeff introduced him as Professor Guy Moberg.

The professor smiled and shook my hand in greeting. "Pleasure to meet you, Anna. The whole town is talking about you and your deer." He raised his glass in a toast. "To those who speak for the animals with no voices. Cheers."

I took the long-stem glass of burgundy Ellie offered. "Thank you."

Jeff held a snifter of brandy up to the flame, examined the jewel-like topaz liqueur, and thoughtfully answered a question no one asked. "I eat the game I shoot."

"Ah," Ellie said triumphantly. "The animals are the vegetarians, and you're the carnivore."

"Just so!" The professor inclined his head toward us. "I hope you don't mind, but I can assure you, hunting is in the DNA of humankind." His bushy eyebrows rose above the tortoise frame of his eyeglasses. He gestured toward the mounted deer, this time with a gentle smile on his face.

"Think of the mess we'd be in if killing for fun was in the DNA of deer." I shot back. "Imagine the headlines ... 'Predator Deer Terrorize Tewksbury!'"

My gaze lingered on the memento of a once-vital life. The stag, in turn, stared defiantly at another mounted head across the room as if he was defending his section of wall.

"What are you feeling?" Professor Moberg asked. Ellie touched my arm. "She looks at them as family."

Moving closer to the stag, I gazed up at his antlers, winged out, groping for his status in the herd. Another trick of my imagination made its eyes blink.

"Sorrow."

A flicker of empathy crossed the professor's eyes. "I hope you don't mind my saying," he said, "when you choose your pets, you also choose your problems."

"My dog is a pet, but I can't imagine my dog mounted on a wall; both deserve to live," I said.

Jeff lifted his glass. "Listen, I agree. Blossom is a little doll. You should concentrate on enjoying the time you guys have with her." His gloom and doom statement, as solemn as a matter-of-fact death sentence, irked me. My back stiffened, and I offered up a prayer for the lie I was about to tell. "I've decided to buy a gun."

Jeff regarded me and grinned. "Oh, brother. Please tell me you're kidding?"

"Really. No joke. I'm thinking outside the box on this one."

Professor Moberg furrowed his brow, perplexed. "A proposal worth some merit. But to what end?"

I took a deep breath and gathered myself. "Let's assume I legally buy a rifle. Pay for all licenses and fees—join a club—get a fancy outfit, have my hair done," I was on a roll.

"Stick to the point," Ellie urged.

"Okay." I lingered over the next sip of wine and struggled to make sense of my spontaneous plan.

"In my mind, the hunting license gives me the right to kill a living animal, a deer, for instance. Simply a matter of the sport and the law. Correct?"

"You're serious?" Jeff gulped his drink. "Where's this going?"

"Voila! Now, I become a legal hunter. That's step one. Think about it—"

Ellie interrupted. "No, I get it. What's step two?"

Bless Ellie.

"Let me finish," I continued. "Step two. I'm a lousy shot and miss my targeted doe. Hypothetically, I'm still legally entitled to her body. By law, she's mine—only ... she's alive!"

I paused for effect and to scrutinize each of their expressions. "Or, can she be mine only if she's dead?"

Jeff hit his head in mock astonishment. "I need another drink. Sorry."

"I forgive you," I retorted, my wine glass raised in a mock salute.

The professor appeared amused, but not surprised. "You don't give up easily, do you?"

"Lots of times. Just not this time. Who has the right to pass a law that sells the life of a wild animal?"

"Well," he ventured, "a good question, but I'm not so sure it is an answerable question."

Pino hurried up to me, accompanied by Mary Beth and Katrina, two of the vets who kept tabs on our menagerie of farm animals.

We hugged. "Got a surprise for you," Mary Beth said. "We're going to nominate Blossom for Purina's Pet of the Year award. It's about how people's lives have been enriched because of a specific animal."

Their excitement was catchy. "A contest? I thought Purina was all about domestic animals."

"Bingo!" Katrina said. "Blossom will be the first wild animal ever considered for an award. Plus, the New Jersey Veterinary Committee already cleared her nomination."

More publicity? I struggled to put on a happy face. "Wow, great news." My words sounded leaden, burdened by the anxiety following any publicity about Blossom. A recent newspaper article had resulted in a near-miss disaster between my car and a motorcyclist, "hoping to see Blossom come out of the woods."

And, then there were the people who read about Blossom and wanted the notoriety of bagging her as a trophy.

Mary Beth saw my hesitancy. "Every vet at the clinic thinks she's extraordinary and deserves the award. How she helped you home after you fell down the hill is an incredible story. Think of the positives. People want alternative humane solutions to the over-population of deer. Like wildlife contraception. The timing is perfect."

"We went to the protest march in Princeton," Pino said.

"You were there?" Mary Beth seemed surprised.

He nodded. "Enough was enough. It was about mass slaughter—not hunting. There were hundreds of people, a lot of them carrying signs: 'Ashamed of You,' 'Stop the Slaughter,' and 'Contraception, the Better Alternative.'"

"They introduced us as Blossom's family," I added. "Many people are following her story on the Friends of Deer website."

Mary Beth jumped in. "Exactly. The more people who know about her, the better her chances of survival."

"I agree," Pino said. "We're over-worrying this situation instead of grabbing at the opportunity to be proactive."

"I guess you could always choose to do nothing." Mary Beth glanced from Pino to me. "This is about a friendship between species. Her nomination could turn attention toward promoting that contraception vaccine you talk about. C'mon, guys, the entry cutoff date is soon, and I need three written testimonials and pictures to submit with the application. Are you in?"

"Okay." Pino took my hand. "You, me, and—who else?"

"I'll bet Jeanne would write something nice."

A small chorus near the piano was doing their best to harmonize the music of the simple yet eloquent Christmas carol.

"Silent night, holy night, All is calm, all is bright ..."

The gentle song offered solace and the right words to explain my feelings. I gazed up at the stag and felt my heart ache.

★ ★ ★

"Sleep in heavenly peace ... Sleep in heavenly peace."

Chapter 19

The Scent of Happiness

"*Neahhh ...*"

I woke up fast on the over-stuffed window seat, where, for the better part of the night, I drifted in and out of listening. The dreamy yawn-like squeal melding with early morning chirps and chit-chat meant only one thing.

Baby!

Pino was out of bed. "Sounds nearby." He pushed aside the sheer curtains so we could peer into the secluded alcove. Beneath the bay window, within the cusp of a thick azalea hedge, Blossom lay curled around her fawn.

She looked up at us with weary yet contented eyes.

"*Aehh...*"

It's been said that in the dark pool of a deer's eyes, there are spirits that call out to certain people. All you have to do is listen. This was one of those times.

Pino tapped the glass and snuffled a bit before his full-blown smile won out. "*Aehh* ... to you too."

I shook his hand. "Are you ogling?" He hesitated, "*Hmm?*"

"I swear, you're like an ogling father at the window of a hospital nursery."

"Let's go," Pino said. "I'll slice up an apple." He called over his shoulder. "What if she doesn't want us near her baby?"

"Of course she does," I hoped.

To me, spring always struggled to get started in March, got drenched in April, and, with a sense of relief, relaxed when it all came together—green, lush, and perfect in May—just in time for the latest bit of awesome in Mother Nature's nursery.

In our pajamas, we hurried outside, tiptoeing through the fragrant, moist grass into the garden. Blossom had braced the newborn against her and was busily bonding; her nose and tongue were probing the tiny mouth and backside, stimulating its senses.

"It's a girl!" Pino laughed when its smooth flat belly was exposed.

We would call her Sweet Pea.

Years ago, I believed it might be too late to start a business, lure Pino away from the corporate New York City spin, and live on a farm we daydreamed about. As diffused light tipped the foliage around us, the dream promised to become more than anything I could have imagined.

The baby tried to rise; she wiggled against her mother's side before plopping over. The array of white spots over her dark caramel fur swirled like dollops of whipped cream in a cup of cocoa.

"She's a scrappy little thing. Have you ever seen such beautiful coloring?" Pino shared the last bite of apple with Blossom.

She took a deep, satisfying breath of her adorable baby. Contented, she closed her eyes and rested.

Love and pride filled me, made even more poignant when I thought of the terrible start Blossom had, alone in the paddock, close to death. Great genetics and survival instincts only got you so far in life. Sometimes, you need a helping hand.

Over the next few days, we saw the devotion deepen between mother and infant. Touch by touch—sniff by sniff—feeling by feeling. Each morning, Blossom brought her fawn to nap beneath the lacy Japanese maple she usually went to when we were in the office. She cocked her head, a familiar quizzical expression on her face, and watched us.

I puffed out a sigh and successfully restrained the urge to go to them—the first time. "Aw ... lovely," I said and tried to get back to work.

"They need some private time, don't you think?" Pino asked. "There's a reason for visiting hours in maternity wards."

I half expected her to want privacy with the baby, too. "See? She's not hiding."

"We hover over them like honeybees around a hive," Pino softened his answer with a half-smile. A sure sign he was caving. "Make sure you leave some berries for tonight's dessert, okay?"

The fawn was awake, perky, tilting her delicately sculpted head this way and that. I knelt and chose a juicy blackberry from the bowl.

Blossom ruled at the berry toss-and-catch, even while lying down. "One for you," I said. She caught it and waited for the next go-round.

"One for me." I opened my mouth wide, maneuvering to catch the big berry coming fast at my face. It bounced off my nose and hit the ground. I could have "kissed it up to God" to sanitize it, a piece of ecumenical advice that struck me as hilarious. Blossom scooped it off the grass, satisfied with her win.

I tossed another. "Catch."

She did, got up, and nudged the fawn under her to nurse.

★ ★ ★

For a few weeks, Blossom stayed nearby but made no attempt to come inside. Often, she would leave her baby under the maple tree and come up to visit, or she would nudge her brush off the windowsill, signaling for her "spa treatment."

Once, when the tiny baby trotted up the path toward us, I think I heard Blossom groan.

"Ah-oh. Guess who's coming for dinner?" I said.

No longer wobbly on gangly legs, Sweet Pea trotted toward her mother, her shiny coat glistening like a caramel candy apple.

"Hey, kiddo, you're all wrapped up in sunshine."

As if she were marching to the beat of a high-stepping band, her front legs energetically marked time with each powerful slurp of milk. This baby had brilliance, rhythm, and a viselike grip on her mother's teat.

"*Aehh* ..."

A comical expression of surprise and bewilderment crossed Blossom's face. She held her head forward but tilted back slightly as if sniffing the air for trouble. For a second, she clamped her eyes on mine, then, with a deft sidestep, pulled her udder out of range.

"*Neahhh ... neahhh ...*" the fawn whined, incensed by the rejection.

Blossom studied her baby, then glanced over at me. For help?

"What?"

Amused, I bent to the fawn. "Hey, Sweet Pea, little vampire fawn, slow down." Cupping her tiny face in my hand, I drew my thumb over her lips. She had the same black over white facial markings as most of the whitetails in our area. "You're not going for the championship, you know."

Standing at attention with all four legs as straight as drumsticks, she studied me with baby-bluish eyes of innocence. The soft lick of her tongue on my hand melted my heart.

I left the two of them and headed down to the barn to feed the horses and alpacas. As I walked, a large doe and her twin fawns came into view on the slope behind the pool fence. I recognized this doe; she was older, with gray hair encircling her peculiar bulging eyes. Her body had a sallow appearance. The fact that she had survived another year was a testament to the hunters' focus on trophy-quality deer.

Caught between a smile and tears, I called to her. "Claire?"

"*Aehh* ..." Blossom trotted past me to greet her friend. Their noses touched. Heads and necks entwined, they seemed to hug. Why not say what I saw?

They did hug.

Chapter 20

Bait

A group of bicyclists whizzed around the corner, chased by grotesquely elongated shadows, unaware that Blossom and I were just a stone's throw from the road. No surprise. Most people wouldn't notice—unless you moved.

The warm air under the leafy maple held close the aromas of newly mown grass, richly composted earth, and a whiff of lilac. At first, I regarded the action as a popcorn spectator, and then, in awe at the miniature version of the tree, and me, in Blossom's globe-like eyes.

She nudged the basket in my lap.

"Okay, here." Gently, she took two cherries from my hand, chewed slowly, and spit out the pits, one at a time, the way you're supposed to. My mind flashed to how many cherry pits I must have swallowed in my lifetime. No stomach aches, yet. I popped one in my mouth, leaned back on my elbows. Spitting out the pit felt right.

"*Eeech*!" I twisted my face away. "You're slurping on my eardrum." Her licks felt fine on my skin since it was warm weather. Cold weather grooming kisses from Blossom could be brutal.

"Want a chip?" The foil bag split with a pop!

"*Aehh* ..." She dug for the dark red chips, her favorites, and crunched loudly.

In sync, like the audience at a tennis match, our heads swung back and forth as a series of runners passed from right to left. Grunts and thumping feet on the tar and chip road—joggers coming from the opposite direction, most with a nod and the universal 'thumbs up!' greeting for fellow enthusiasts.

"*Pssst.* Nancy. Over here," I signaled. She allowed the runners to pass, and made a simple U-turn on the grass, without losing a beat.

"Hiya, Anna. Hey, Blossom. Where's Sweet Pea?" She tweaked Blossom's ears, backed away from the branches, and started the routine drill that kept her fit: stretching out her shoulders, hamstrings, quads, swinging high, scooping low between her legs, lunging, twisting.

I gestured toward the house. "Asleep in the garden. Geez, I'm exhausted just watching you. If I did that, I'd break."

"I was going to call you later. People are setting up a deer blind on the strip of woods upstream from your paddock."

I stared at her, remembering that buffer zone as a soggy crisscrossed mesh of downed trees and thick vegetation. *Stay focused.* I coughed to clear the knot in my throat. "How did you find out?"

★ ★ ★

Nancy shuffled in place, flushed from her workout. "Robin was planting a new bed of day lilies in her rock garden when she saw people unloading a hunting tree stand on that vacant property across from her house."

"Who are they?"

She hesitated. "Didn't say, but she made them promise not to shoot the deer with the collar, or her baby." Nancy put her hands on her hips and bent forward into another stretch.

"One guy gave Robin a story about hunting to protect the undergrowth on Wildwood Road. She says, they knew all about Blossom. Even joked about using her as bait!"

Prickles of fear surged up my neck. "Bait?" Protectively, I touched Blossom's hip.

"How?"

She rolled her eyes. "You're kidding? For starters, she's the only deer with a collar, her poster is hanging all over the place, and she comes to people who call her. The other deer will follow her right into their trap.

"They'll be easy targets. Last year a kid bragged about shooting a fawn and a doe. Illegal or not, no one did anything about it."

She wiped the beads of sweat from her face and knelt beside Blossom. "I dare someone to tell me the logic behind some people teaching kids to kill a sweet, defenseless animal, like you." She kissed her nose, looked at me. "I suppose it would start something like, 'Look at them as I see them, son— no more than robotic ducks on a conveyor belt at a country fair.'"

"Don't get me started."

"Damn it, Nancy, no matter how great things are going, it seems like we're under attack. That land is too close. Kids play there. How can that be legal? Besides being designated wetland, swampy, and probably full of snakes!"

She glanced at me, surprised. "And, you think that matters to people looking for a hunting thrill? Anyway, they're going to start baiting the deer early to prep for the season.

"I'm running a five-mile circuit. I'll try to find out more."

Several joggers passed, and she picked up her pace behind them.

I found no solace in watching Blossom, her head deep in the crinkly veggie chip bag, looking for the last licks of salty crumbles. The reality of the logistics—a narrow strip of land, no wider than a golf fairway, bordered by homes and paddocks, could become a killing field.

My hands were sweaty, and my heart ached with the same helpless anger, familiar to people who have been unlucky enough, at one time or another, to be stilted by the more powerful.

Use Blossom as a lure? And what about little Sweet Pea? Would they grab her first? Blossom would fight—she is not a quitter.

I'm not a quitter either.

We needed answers.

It took concentration and time. Pino and I worked long hours creating our Leather Therapy product brand, which was gaining international acclaim. I was writing and filing for a patent, but the distant hammering from the hunting site pounded like a ticking time bomb in my ears, sending my creative juices down the drain.

Within days, Nancy found the name of the property owner, a retired dentist named Witherspoon, and info about plans for "a hunting and bonding experience for the family."

My attempts to contact Witherspoon met with silence and more sleepless nights, plagued by the ways Blossom could be set up as bait. Shot or not, the experience of being caught in a killing field would terrify her, as it would any sensitive living being.

She could be gone in a blink, and her life won't stand for anything except a metaphor of powerlessness or, perhaps, a headline.

Antsy to scope out the preparations for the fall ambush of our local whitetails, I made up my mind. "Pino, I want to see what's happening. Meanwhile, I'm writing Witherspoon again. How does 'legality shouldn't replace humanity' sound?"

"Good luck with that approach. Online, there's a picture of five dead young bucks, lined up like sardines—"

"Don't tell me."

* * *

Digital clocks never let you forget the exact time. 12:28 A.M.— 1:47 a.m.—2:53 a.m.

The rain had stopped. Unusually chilly gray and drippy weather rolled over the eastern seaboard, forecast to clear out by mid-morning. I doubled the pillows behind my back, adjusted the clip-on book light, and tried to lose myself in a cozy mystery. I looked at Pino.

How does he do it? Within a nanosecond of the lights dimming, he was in dreamland.

"*Aehh*!" Blossom's wailing scream cut through the night, and the distinctive sound of a plastic bucket bouncing down the front steps.

Blossom! There were reports of a bear in the area. I threw back the blanket, ran to the foyer, flipped on the lights, and swung open the door.

"Wait!" Waking up as fast as he fell asleep, Pino was close behind and grabbed my walking stick.

On her hind legs, Blossom's impressive six-foot body was ready for battle. Enraged, pawing the air and snorting, her eyes locked on whatever was terrorizing her. She attacked the small bucket, slamming it once, twice, against the steps with her front feet.

Bang!

Small, scrambling and scratching noises came from inside, and the triangular fuzzy white face of a terrified young possum peeked out.

"No, no." Pino held his hands up to calm Blossom.

"Aw, come on. It's just a possum. A dizzy little possum," I said, watching the pointy white face of the animal stumble back into the bucket for safety—a wrong choice.

"Watch out; its teeth are razor sharp." Pino lifted the pail with the stick and carried it to the grass.

Blossom now was more interested in the curious critter shuffling away, its rat-like tail wobbling into the blackness. Then, she headed for the garden and Sweet Pea.

Back in the kitchen, I switched on the electric kettle and opened a box of almond biscotti for dunking. "Want hot tea?" I stirred two spoons of raw honey into steaming cups of Earl Grey and headed for the soft leather couch in the den where we could sit cozy, content, and relaxed in the wonderful feeling of being tired.

Pino closed his eyes. "If you don't sleep, you're going to get sick. I know, I know. It's about the hunting blind."

"Yeah ..." I held the warm cup close to my face and inhaled the soothing bittersweet aroma. "... I'm fine."

He paused. "Bad dreams?"

"Same ole—same ole—I'm a helpless victim. Struggling to see, to move, but I can't. Makes me feel sickish."

He was quiet, and his hand, equally still, rested on my knee.

"It's a sort of standard 'no control' nightmare, don't you think? As a kid, I was always running or fighting someone in my sleep."

"At least you had enough sense to fight back. Ever win?"

"After a few years." A slight smile flickered over his face. We lapsed into a long silence.

Pino spread his hands around the hot mug. "You're only a victim in your mind," he said. "No one sees you like that."

"Yeah, my secret," I said. "Being bullied hurts. My brain needs re-programming, a thorough overhaul, and a good lube job. On the other hand, I think a lot of my caring comes from losing those battles."

"So, what did you mean about being bullied?"

"It's ridiculous," I said.

It was strange that night. It was close to 4:00 a.m., and I was half asleep, prepared to unload a memory, still locked and loaded in my mind.

"You want to listen to a dumb story about the Girl Scouts?"

"Go for it," he said.

I sighed. "The Girl Scout motto is 'Be prepared,' but I wasn't on that day ..."

"I'm listening."

"So, our small group of uniformed scouts was late boarding the bus for the YMCA pool. I wanted to earn the swimming badge, but I forgot to pack a shirt and stayed back to talk to our scout leader. 'Do you have a tee shirt I can wear? I get cold,' I lied. "Pamela was busy and brushed me off with a smile. 'The pool is heated,' she said.

"It was difficult—I didn't know how to speak up—to ask for help. 'But, but, I'm burned,' I finally blurted. I trusted her to understand.

'Nobody will notice. You worry too much for a kid. Go on now; we're late.'

"I wanted to die.

"The only vacant seat had ripped green vinyl with sharp edges. I sat on my notebook so that it wouldn't pinch and stared through the grimy, sun-streaked bus window the entire ride.

"Know what's funny?" I asked him. "Ha-ha, funny?"

I shook my head. "No. Strange funny.

"I can still see my toes curled so tight over the edge of the pool they turned white and hear echoing little-girl screeches fill the domed room. Mary was in a circle with the other Scouts and called me to come in. Imagine something as inconsequential as that staying with you for life?

"The pool was warm—I knew, as warm as bath water, but I was shivering, frozen with fear—but unwilling to give up the pink towel covering me.

"'You're not listening.' Pamela unwrapped me. 'Be brave, go on in. Go!' I took a deep breath before jumping. My eyes burned from chlorine as I swam underwater."

"*Hmm* ... understandable. Good for you, though," Pino said. "It didn't take long to get noticed."

I would not talk about the pretty, blond girl who kinda poked at me and squealed, "She's a freaky fish." The expression on her face hurt more than anything else.

"A few skinny-armed Scouts, who I thought were my friends, splashed slabs of water at my head, driving me toward the deep end of the pool. I remember being fascinated at how the water sloshed in and out of their bathing suits.

"'Leave me alone!' I slapped water back at the girl who poked me and prayed to God to make me vanish.

'Take it easy.' Someone grabbed my arm.

"'STOP!' Pamela demanded. They did. At the side of the pool, I grabbed for the towel as if it were a life preserver.

"Pamela put her hand on my head and held me as I cried. 'They don't mean it.'

"The tears were no longer about my scars but for the realization that hoping to 'not be different' was a wasted emotion, as were the lies that urged me to believe that they could be true. I put my head between my legs and coughed up the water bubbling from my lungs."

Pino asked softly. "Those voices from the past still whisper to you in the middle of the night? How old is that memory?"

I took another long sip of tea. "You into carbon dating?" I grinned but still felt sad for the hurt child in my story.

"I think everyone experiences bullying in some way, at some point in their lives. You are who you are—caring comes from losing those battles you still dream about. Blossom is who she is because you're in her life. You're both better for that."

I slept until noon the next day.

Chapter 21

Booby Trap

Pino tapped the windowpane before opening the tack room door. "What's up? Those your anti-snake boots?"

From my seat on the trunk, I shoved my feet into knee-high rubber muck boots. "Got that right. So, am I being foolish?"

"Foolish? You?" He put my walking stick inside the door, his eyes full of concern. "This might come in handy. I'm going with you."

The small creek bordering the paddock prevented the ground in the southeastern corner of Unicorn Hollow from drying out completely. It trickled over smooth river rocks most of the time but could churn violently into a flood zone after a heavy downpour. Each squishy step released woodsy aromas of mushrooms, mosses, and composting vegetation.

"Hold my hand." Pino navigated us through the boggy ground and half-buried branches. Fat toads called incessantly in low-pitched trills, like idling diesel engines. Plopping to safety through puddles when they heard us coming, wide-eyed gazing, stare for stare.

"Yuck. Creepy." We played tug-of-war with the ground. "Like walking on a live worm farm. You know, those cutaway glass tanks they sell for kids?"

"This is nuts. Next time, we come the easy, normal way from the road," he grunted. "Deep here ... go slow ... wiggle your feet." Suddenly, he stopped, struggled for balance, and started to fall.

"Let go of my hand!" he twisted out of his boot and clutched a fallen tree trunk blanketed with shelves of semi-circular mushrooms. An iridescent blue-bellied newt stood its ground for a second, then, with a flick of its tail, took cover on the backside of a stump.

"*Oompf!*" Pino pulled his way to the tree, one bootless foot held high behind.

"Don't move," I said.

Disgusted, he grumbled, "Don't move? "I can't move."

"It's stuck." I rocked the boot until the suction broke with a loud, sloppy sucking noise. I passed the mess to Pino. "Here ya go, Sweetness. The ground burped it up."

"This isn't working." He used his sock to remove green gunk from his face and shoved his foot back into the boot. "I give up."

"In a week, we'll remember to laugh about this."

"You're not serious." He wasn't laughing.

"There it is!" I pointed at the dark object at least twenty feet off the ground, surrounded by hardwood trees. We made our way into the clearing, about the size of Justinian's round pen, and acquainted ourselves with the deadly side of animal conservation.

Sweet clumps of Lily of the Valley and long grass grew haphazardly, and curly ferns hugged a few trees on the far side, closest to the stream. Tree-trunk benches were placed around the perimeter, and the ground was prepared like an amphitheater, complete with gallery seats for spectators.

Sharp pointy tracks of deer, some deeper and broader, intermingled with indentations from new fawns and does. There were plenty of hunting stands and blinds within the tracts of woods and fields surrounding Tewksbury. But nothing like this one.

"Well, la-di-da ... wonderful, just wonderful," I sarcastically remarked.

"Will you take a gander at this outfit?" Pino checked the mechanism, pulley, and haul ropes dangling from an industrial-sized hook screwed into the tree. "Wonder what this is for?"

I drew a deep, desperate breath at the deadly slickness of it all. "Like the gallows—for a deer carcass ..." I felt my throat constrict. I'd had it with the arrogance of this so-called civilized sport.

"This setup must have cost plenty." He nodded, ducking behind the ladder to study the underbelly of the platform and feeder.

"Lucky, lucky," I blurted. "Last chance to evaluate this crème de la crème, five-star-rated hunting blind. Suitable especially for those select individuals who want to enjoy the good life, have a little schnapps, in as much luxury as can be eked out of a tree stand."

"You sound like an auctioneer," Pino said.

"You got it." I rattled on in a mocking tone. "But wait, there's more. On sale now, a worry-free baiter will release pre-packaged corn or pelleted food so that *your* deer has the robust, unmistakable look of vitality—when you kill it."

Pino's fingers traced the black battery wire around the inside edge of the mechanism. "Yeah, these people have money to spend. If only I could understand why they don't see the beauty of life in the animals they kill. 'Blind' is the right word for it."

"We could spray the ground with deer repellant, I suppose—maybe hot pepper. Remember the hot sauce recipe that kept Blossom away from our azaleas?"

"Yup, the same hot sauce that Caruso couldn't get enough of," Pino said. "I mostly remember the cost to replace the windowsill he ate as an appetizer. Even if we disable the feeder temporarily."

"Worth a shot." I yanked the wire free and left it swinging.

Pino frowned, annoyed. "What on earth are you thinking?"

I tried to crush a small pile of corn into the ground. "Look at what we're up against. Don't you realize how difficult this is going to be?" I knew he cared as deeply as I did. "Sorry." So much for my law-abiding, moral compass going haywire.

"Listen." He waved the detached end of the cable. "We can get in trouble for this. Do you want to give away any leverage we already have?" He wiped his brow, leaving a trail of muddy streaks across his face.

I had been thinking just that. "Now what? Witherspoon won't return my calls—people don't change. Something terrible is going to happen. We're doomed, and so are Blossom and Sweet Pea. End of story."

"I'm with you." He turned his attention back to the wire and rolled it between his fingers, studying the frayed end. "We'll see. Give me a minute."

The clearing was also full of life. Birds, squirrels, and a few chipmunks darted in and out of the corn bonanza. I sat on a log tucked into a recess opposite the blind, gazed up, past the trees, into the sky, and then down at the surprise of rose-striped Lady Slipper orchids growing a few feet from where I sat. As if masquerading as a lineup of courtesans sharing a secret, they appeared poised within their deep pink pouches and broad green leaves. As stately as flowers at a funeral.

"Finished." Pino trudged over and sat next to me.

"Suppose I create a decoy of sorts," I said. "Something that gets attention ... like hanging Blossom's poster up there." I pointed to a tall oak closest to the stand. "Or, over there, high up, across from that log? Perhaps we can convince a few people that a photograph and a kiss from a live deer is a thousand times better and more exciting than a slew of grinning faces over a dead trophy deer."

"Somewhat melodramatic, don't you think?" Pino looked at me with a wry grin.

My spirits were rising at the merits of the idea. "Blossom can't speak for herself. Our posters could be more like a community service announcement."

"Spoken like a born rescuer. That's sure thinking outside the box." He stood to go.

"At least, it's something. Damn, to kill just for the fun of it is as cruel as it gets. I need some gimmick to tickle the imagination." I studied the robotic feeder. "That gizmo is set to rotate every few hours, I suppose. Nothing we can do about it." I took his hand.

"*Ouch*!" He winced but seemed surprisingly upbeat and smug. There was a huge smile on his face.

"Did you get hurt when you fell? What's so funny?"

"It got caught up in the rotary unit back there. Didn't hurt."

"It got caught?"

He glanced around. "Let's just say that the food timer may be malfunctioning for a while."

"You jimmied it?" I laughed, switched sides, and squeezed his good hand.

Within a week, six new waterproof posters dotted the trees around the hunters' blind. I staggered them, high and low, so as not to overlap obtrusively, as the old billboards along highways did. They were certainly obvious—in a discreet, sort of classy way. Pleased yet aware that my actions could open a hornet's nest of controversy that might backfire, I returned the next day to spray a deer-repellant mixture under the baiter.

I wanted the clearing to be vacant—peaceful—but knew what would be there.

"NO, NO, NO! Get away!" I ran at them, waving my arms wildly. Whitetails scattered like spindrift blown from the crest of a breaking ocean wave.

All except one.

With an effort, I remained still, then dropped to my knees. "Blossom! Why won't you listen to me? You have to stay away from here!" As I spoke, her keen eyes never left mine, barely blinked. She took in every word, every emotion, and listened quietly.

"*Aehh* ..." She came close and reached to kiss my face with a gesture of such affection it took my breath away. I criss-crossed my arms over her back and felt the pulse of her heart in my chest. "Blossom, can you feel my heart like I can feel yours? Remember this hug, okay? Your heart and mine—in the middle."

Doom and gloom, twin attitudes, stayed with me for days. My efforts to shake things up with frequent visits to the deer blind accomplished a big fat zero.

"How am I supposed to scare them away when Blossom shows up to say hi," I said to Pino. "Today, she and Sweet Pea came running to greet me."

My plan had irritated somebody. All but one of the posters had been pulled down by the next weekend, and the automatic feeder was dropping bait again. Strangely, the poster closest to the blind was still there, nailed to the tree.

When I returned to the house at dusk, I flipped on the kitchen lights. A red LED signaled a new message on the answering machine.

"Hello, this is Eric Witherspoon, your neighbor. Sorry, I didn't call you earlier. Um, I think we have to have a conversation about your deer."

The long pause led me to expect the worst. I bit my bottom lip and held my breath in preparation for the verbal ax to fall—wasted energy. The message continued in a spirit of congeniality.

"Let's see if we can't save Blossom."

"Yes!"

Chapter 22

A Matter of Perspective

L ucky me.

Today was going to be a vibrant and frisky day. I felt it. Nature seemed to think so, too. From grand old trees towering umbrella-like over the roads of Tewksbury to minuscule flowers bursting from the tiniest mosses below. All free for those who cared to notice.

Earlier, I saw Blossom lingering near the far side of the mailbox until the yellow school bus and the two girls blowing kisses to her through half-opened windows were out of sight.

"Good morning, Blossom." I crossed the lawn. A lush patch of grass held her attention for the time being. Dilly-dallying her way in front of a line of tall pines, backlit by strobe-like rays from the intense sun, she intermittently glowed a ripe-apricot color, then black in silhouette, like an animated flip book from an old-fashioned penny arcade.

Swirls of biting no-see-ums swarmed above Blossom's head like mini-dust devils. She ducked, flicked her tail, and shivered her silky skin to shake them off. For just such a day, my pockets were loaded with treats and bug repellent wipes.

Once again, our mailman had done the impossible with rubber bands and packed our mailbox to what Pino called "torque velocity." The artsy mailbox, hand-painted with bright yellow sunflowers, had country charm. As usual, its black metal door served as a platform for the overflow of the day's mail.

I shook open one of the catalogs and made a big deal of waving it, as active a signal as a flag drop at the start of a race. Blossom was eager for our mail-game to start. She bounded over in delight.

"*Aehh* ..." She greeted me with a bump to my leg. Front legs tucked against her chest, she chomped down, pulling at the edge of a magazine, until the mail lay scattered around us.

"You must have been practicing. What a mess." I gathered the mail and opened a padded envelope stamped Do Not Bend. The gummy flap peeled back smoothly.

"Uh-oh!" A dent near the edge of the thick parchment diploma-like certificate bore the New Jersey Veterinary Association seal, Animal Hall of Fame, and "Blossom," in beautiful calligraphic lettering, written across the front.

"Woohoo! Blossom, you've got mail." I waved the bent certificate over my head. "From the Pet of the Year contest. Absolutely suitable for framing."

Blossom did one of her full-body rumbling shakes, her ears flapping like the beating wings of birds. She followed me into the house to show Pino, rumbling down the carpeted staircase to the office, three steps at a time.

"Sounds like I'm at the bottom of Niagara Falls. Either that or a rock slide," Pino said.

"Did she win?" He tried to smooth the creases out of the parchment by re-rolling it on his desk. I read the cover letter.

"A K-9 dog unit won for their search and rescue efforts during the World Trade Center disaster, a parrot named Murphy who helps an Alzheimer's patient, and a dog working with children at a school for the deaf took the Place and Show categories. But she got Special Recognition."

Pino made a big deal over the award. "Oooh, Blossom. Only true champions ever achieve Special Recognition."

Blossom's tail wagged with delight at the attention.

"Where should we hang it?" He held the certificate against the brick wall near my desk. "Heads up, sweetness. The celebrity is eating pretzels off your desk."

★ ★ ★

Coincidence? I don't think so. I find it fascinating when unrelated events and ideas merge, re-energizing strategies and bringing new people into our lives.

Mark Fraker phoned from Victoria, Canada. "We've done the science, legwork, and field testing on the contraception vaccine, and now I've got to convince some people at the federal level to provide monetary support. I'm meeting with the Bureau of Land Management and any senators that will hear me out next Monday in Washington."

I heard an almost imperceptible sigh. "And, something else. Without government help to subsidize the SpayVac program, it's not going to happen."

"I'm driving our trailer with a few alpacas to my sister's farm, an hour west of Washington on Saturday."

He hesitated briefly. "Well then, perfect timing. Would you like to attend the meetings with me? You'll learn a lot."

"Me?"

"Sure. Bring Blossom's picture."

My only clue to what Mark looked like was the photograph on the inside cover of the small book he wrote. I pulled it off my shelf and studied the tall, lanky man bundled in a sealskin parka, surrounded by an eclectic group of like-minded people engrossed in a life and death battle to open a frozen passageway to the sea for a family of trapped whales.

The plans were finalized. We would stay at my sister's farm in The Plains, Virginia. Mary had given an enthusiastic "see ya on the flip-flop" to the visit.

The ruby-red morning sun reached halfway down our barn's roof, the street was fading to violet, and my two-horse trailer was packed and ready to transport six alpacas to their new digs in the rolling hills of Virginia's horse country.

★ ★ ★

Pino removed the center divider, hung a new hay bag on a hook above the back-window grid, and fluffed up piles of clean-smelling straw for bedding to make the four-hour drive easier on the animals.

"Blossom," I called, hoping her sensitive sonar-like hearing would pick up my voice. I scanned the outer edges of the paddocks and waited, then went back to re-check the alpacas.

Behind the round pen, I saw her jump over the rock wall, bolt across two paddocks, and leap over the fence behind the barn. The horses and alpacas didn't bother to look up.

She brushed against me on her way to check out the trailer.

"Aehh ..."

"Good morning, girly."

Always curious, she jumped inside, pulled a clump of alfalfa hay out of the feeder, and circled down next to the front wall, getting comfortable around the telltale bulge of another pregnancy.

"Honestly, Blossom, another baby?" I climbed into the dim, comfy space. "Move over." I shimmied down, my fingers interlocked behind my head for support. Outside the double loading doors, all was sunny, bright, and green, like the light at the end of a tunnel.

Pino must have forgotten—leather reins from Justinian's bridle still hung over the hay bag. Why, after all these years, could a fleeting glance at a long strap of leather send a shiver up my spine as a reminder of my father's belt?

Blossom nudged my leg, and I forgot about it. We were as content with each other as close friends should be.

I talked to her about everything but nothing in particular, all the while making an effort to remember the little details of her beautifully expressive eyes, straight black lashes, the dip starting at the inner corners and curving down to the puffiness below when she didn't sleep well. I stroked the strip of white fur above her leathery nose and the soft, velvety skin at the base of her ears.

All the while, she stayed alert with one ear tuned to the world outside, the other on my voice. Blossom was an excellent listener. Lulled into silence by the drowsy atmosphere in the boxy little trailer, I thought of the dull gray pickup rattling by the farm yesterday, the body of a young buck tied to its tailgate, and the moaning sounds that night from the deer, almost like humans, grieving.

I gazed at my sweet friend, wondering if every goodbye would turn out to be the final farewell. My mom used to say, "Don't waste a good worry until you know the facts." I had the facts, so I was worried.

"It's only for a few days, just a short visit." It occurred to me I was giving myself permission to leave her. "Did one of your friends die? Are you sad?"

Blossom tilted her head toward me, seemingly responsive to the tone and emotion in my voice. She moistened her nose with her tongue.

"Listen, I have a plan. The first step is to give you the birth control vaccine, so you don't have any more babies. What? You don't think I can do it?" I teased. "Come on. We're a team, you know? I want you to under- stand something. Even though you like people, not everybody is your friend." I held her head to prove I was serious.

"That creepy guy making the phone calls is back. But now he's leaving threatening messages to scare us. He says he can kill you whenever he feels like it." I shuddered a moment at the thought of his call.

"*Aehh* ..."

"How many times have I told you to stay away from creepy guys, huh?"

I pulled a new pink satin ribbon from my pocket and dangled it in front of her. "Here, I have something for you." She nosed it. I flipped my ponytail toward her. "The other half is here in my hair, see? This one's for you." I tied the wide ribbon into an elegant bow on the back of her collar, knotted it twice, and thought of the pink satiny ribbon my mother brought to my hospital bed so many years before as a sign of love.

A warm, gusty breeze swooshed through the grated windows, loose strands of hay rustled in the feeders, and the bridle reins swayed and dropped a few inches from the hook. The forecast called for light rain.

"Ah-choo," I sneezed loudly.

Suddenly, Blossom stood and snorted in alarm. "Oops, sorry."

She was terrified. The hair on her neck and back stood straight up, her eyes staring—up, down, to the side, back at me, as if she was looking for an escape route. But something else was wrong. A frosty trickle of fear crossed my shoulders.

"*Aehhhh*!" Blossom screamed in an unusually throaty rumble.

The breeze had stopped—but, then, what was it? I rolled to my right, and froze, grasping for some hidden strength to dismiss the dark form lurking at the edge of my peripheral vision that started to sway—curl—and angle up.

I knew with the disabling terror I had imagined in every nightmare since childhood. Knew with certainty what the thick strap, suspended as a ropy silhouette across the back entrance had to be—a snake.

"*Aaaah!*"

The trailer rocked as I scrambled to get up, my sweaty palms groping for stability on the shiny-white composite wall. I slipped, once, twice, in the deep straw bedding.

The snake swayed, but never lost its focus on us.

Think. Think. Think!

As a paramedic, I learned to identify distinctive patterns of a snake's skin. But that was in Florida. This snake was not the "black on yellow, kill a fellow" coral snake type. It was not a notorious pit-viper, like the golden-headed copperhead, with heat-sensing pits between its eyes and nostrils. This one was jet black, with a bright red ring encircling its neck.

Farmers told me black snakes are not venomous, eat rats, are usually non-aggressive, and can be several feet in length. "They're your friends," they said.

A long, slender muscle. Red band around its neck. And, curious.

No one ever mentioned anything about curiosity.

Blossom stepped back as the snake coiled into a bow-like shape, extending into the compartment. Its red, forked tongue flicked ... sniffing.

We were trapped. *Where is my walking stick when I need it?*

Blossom took a tentative step toward the snake.

Intermittent puffs of wind whistled through the windows— the snake now swaying at Blossom's eye level, its beetle-black eyes fixed on her. I was wary but trusted her natural balance of guts and instincts. We needed to get outside, into the sunshine, into the sweet meadow scent of the grass. I stared in disbelief as Blossom stretched even closer.

"Blossom, don't." She didn't listen.

If I hadn't become so unglued, I might have seen some humor in the scene that followed.

The snake arched its head toward Blossom, then swung back toward me.

Growing up in the hospital I had been told, "If you can change your perspective, you can change your attitude." I was ready to give it a try.

"Hey, you over there," I said to the snake. Blossom's left ear rotated toward me; then she gave me one of her "don't do this to me" looks.

"I know for a fact black snakes are 'my friends,' so I'm going to call you Faccia-brutta. It means something like 'ugly face' in Italian. No offense.

"Here's the deal, Faccia-brutta. Blossom and I are leaving, so don't get any funny ideas in your little snake brain." My confidence was growing, and I decided to be nice. "By the way, somebody must love you 'cause you're wearing a pretty red collar around your neck. Blossom has a collar."

"Aehh ..."

Blossom was waiting for me to act. In one swift motion, I leaned on her, scooped a mound of straw from the floor, and hurled it at the snake. Bull's eye! The snake hissed and recoiled before flinging itself to the floor.

"Go!"

Blossom jumped over the snake and bounded out of the trailer. Three steps and a short jump to the ground landed me on the grass behind her. I scrambled to my feet, and we hightailed it up the hill to the office. "Pino!"

"Where was the snake?" Pino asked. "In the hay bag."

"The hay bag I put up?"

"Yeah, you did it."

"Crap!" Pino shouted and shuddered.

"She could have run away, but stood her ground," I told him. "I think Faccia-brutta was just as scared of us, right Blossom? Maybe he got hissy because he didn't like his name." I passed her a blueberry.

Pino picked up a book of East Coast maps and highlighted the route to Mary's new farm in Virginia. "You should be on the road before noon tomorrow. You'll have plenty of time to get the animals settled, unhitch the trailer, and get to the airport. Wish I was going with you."

A few minutes later, Pino started for the trailer armed with a rake, on which he intended to transport Faccia-brutta to a safe zone off our property.

It was after eleven when I finally pulled out of the driveway with the little trailer loaded with six alpacas, a lot of optimism, and a plan to help save the whitetails. Legally.

Snake-less, we headed for Virginia.

Chapter 23

Cedar Hill Farm

The Dulles Airport arrival gate was crowded, but there was no mistaking the tall, lanky Canadian wearing a vest with pockets everywhere and a bulky knapsack slung over one arm.

Exactly what I expected a wildlife biologist to look like. From my description, he recognized my car, and an amiable grin lit his face. I don't recall if we ever stopped talking on the hour drive to the farm.

Deep within Virginia's scenic hunt country, the air was fresh. The shaded driveway of Cedar Hill Farm wound past acres of fenced paddocks, a tranquil pond with vivid alpine-blue Adirondack chairs at its edge, and dipped beneath century-old, black walnut trees before curving into a vista of rolling lawns leading to the country estate.

Burnished copper roofs sloped over the eighty-five hundred square foot stone house, opalescent in the mid-afternoon sunshine. Overnight rain had given everything a newly washed feel, and the sun was already warm, promising another splendid day.

"Looks more like a chateau than a farm." Mark focused his camera on a group of fluffy-headed, long-necked animals who stopped grazing to watch our approach. "Never met an alpaca before."

"Well, then this is going to be your lucky day." I grinned at the quizzical expression on his face. "They look a lot like ET aliens for a few months after we shear their fleece." Tinkerbelle, an unusually social alpaca female trained at Unicorn Hollow, with a fondness for carrots and people, awaited our arrival.

Mary waved and crossed the stone entry into the courtyard. "Hey, Sis." She gave me a quick sis-kiss and turned to Mark. "Welcome." She hugged him hard. "Come in and get settled, then I'll take you guys around the place if you're not exhausted. My sister is your biggest fan."

"I'm a fan of hers too, so we're equal. I've never seen anything like her remarkable relationship with Blossom."

Tinkerbelle traipsed after us, intermittently springing into the air, all four feet off the ground, delighted with the attention. "It's called pronking," I said.

He walked ahead to shoot a waterfall cascading over granite boulders into a natural pool, turning this way and that to capture the light, the shadows, and the animals' interactions within their environment.

"That's what naturalists do. We detail nature as photojournalists document the news. Two weeks ago, I was surrounded by barren ice in Alaska." He swept the view with wide open arms. "This lushness is the other end of the spectrum."

"Sis, I could use your help getting the alpacas settled. Want to come?"

Mark asked,"Do I have time before dinner to take a walk around the pond?"

"Sure. Dinner is at 6:30, on the patio," Mary said.

He strolled off, stopping at the bend in the driveway to take a few pictures. It occurred to me that Mark was taking a respite from the worry that would start in earnest tomorrow.

★ ★ ★

From the patio, we followed the progression of long shadows etching away at the lush northern foothills of the Blue Ridge Mountains, where sixty alpacas and a few horses faded into the darkness. Automatic lights blinked on like mini-constellations set between the rock walls of stone terracing.

"Cheers." Wine glasses touched and clinked.

A calico kitten climbed the wisteria-draped pergola and tiptoed her way through a lacy veil of long, blue flowers above the table. "Bailey is always in trouble," Mary said as an assortment of slender petals and leaves fell on the tray of jumbo shrimp. "So much for my elegant candlelight feast."

"Edible flowers?" Mark teased as he reached for another helping.

"*Rreow!*" Faces turned up, and hands went out, too late to stop the inevitable fall.

Bailey's back legs desperately peddled the air above our heads, as if on a stationary exercise bike, seconds before the flash of fur landed in the salad bowl.

"*Rreow!*"

"Good landing, kitty," I said. "Kitten salad, anyone?" Mary asked, her fork halfway to her mouth, as Bailey shook pieces of lettuce from her paws.

I pushed back into the cushiony chair and swirled my wine. "We have common goals here. You need money to keep the SpayVac research going, and we need the program to protect Blossom and control the deer population without slaughter and bullets surrounding us."

He nodded. "We have the potential to solve an important problem humanely, benefiting both animals and humans. I've spent most of the past decade of my forty-year career trying to advance this wildlife contraception idea, and the path has been full of obstacles. Meanwhile, research data keeps proving that a single dose of the vaccine continues to outperform all other contraceptive agents available."

"Can you give Blossom the SpayVac injection soon after she gives birth this year?" I asked. *Did I imagine a slight shake of his head?*

"I wish I could. I'm sorry, it's not possible." His fingers drummed steadily on the table.

"Why not? Doesn't it make sense to publicize the vaccine by following Blossom's journey and our efforts to save her?" I had the awful realization that I had jumped the gun and over-thought the situation. My enthusiasm had gotten me nowhere.

"I realize it means a lot to you," he said. "Keep in mind that the same technology is being used to create the next generation of versatile human vaccines—a much more lucrative side of the business, without all the hullabaloo from the hunting commu-nity. The lab has stopped producing the vaccine for wildlife."

"No! But then, how can Blossom fit into the scenario?"

"Your deer adds a much more personal light to the situation. People are interested in her. The more people are made aware of her story, the easier it will be to secure funding, even through private sources. It can happen."

We spoke late into the evening about Mark's advocacy as an environmental scientist, the Exxon Valdez oil spill, the plight of Africa's elephants, whales, deer, and hunting, and how slow the government moves.

He leaned forward. "There are problems with the compet-itive vaccine to SpayVac. It requires transporting frozen serum, thawing, and mixing components in the field before injecting." He demonstrated by alternating his thumbs over imaginary syringe plungers. "We have one opportunity per animal to make this right.

"Imagine doing this one hundred times for each dose while a wild animal is being held, drugged, or restricted. Plus, protocol requires re-gathering for yearly booster shots. The costs to hire people, gather animals and vaccinate, plus the trauma to wild-life, would be enormous.

"If a vaccine isn't easy to use in the field, it can never be cost-effective. On the positive side, the contraception idea is gaining acceptance amongst biologists and advocacy groups worldwide."

Mark sounded hopeful. "Tomorrow, I'll create some excite-ment, maybe convince someone at the federal level to become an advocate for us. After that happens, we'll need media coverage, the public, and government involvement. Blossom and the wild mustang Cloud would become the faces of the campaign. You've heard of Cloud?"

"Sure, the palomino stallion," Mary said. "Helicopter round-ups. Foals were dying because they couldn't keep up with the herd. I saw the documentary twice. Some, not adopted, were sold for slaughter."

I recalled lots of in-depth reporting and media coverage. The photo spread in Equus magazine called for action with images that broke many hearts. In particular, the anguish in the eyes of a mare and her terrified baby crowded against a fence in the slaughter pen. The horses were sold cheaply to move them off federal land that one of the wealthiest corporations wanted for grazing their cattle.

"So, who's the 'they'?" Mary asked. "Cattle are much more destructive to land. Crazy. Who makes those decisions? I'll bet if you follow the money trail, you'll find out. Isn't that the way it usually turns out?"

Mark nodded. "America loves its horses. Compassion is stronger for horses than deer in this country and could help gain notoriety and funding. Most people don't know about the round-ups. SpayVac can help control both the horse and deer population."

It was after eleven o'clock at night when I phoned Pino and filled him in on the day's events.

"One more thing," Pino chuckled. "This will make you laugh. Blossom made an appearance at an outdoor wedding Jeff and Vivian attended last weekend. You know, the house at the end of Fox Hill with the stand of fir trees?"

"She did what?"

"Jeff said it was surreal. Picture this. The trees were lit with gold lights behind a flower-draped trellis—the bride and groom were taking their vows—when Blossom stepped into the light, only a few yards away. She stood quietly, watching the couple. She blended, except for her reflecting collar. Jeff said he felt like a big uncle and told everyone her name.

"The guests raised their glasses to the couple blessed by Mother Nature herself."

"I wish we could have seen that. Did Blossom nibble the wedding flowers?" I asked, picturing that, too.

"He didn't mention anything about missing flowers. Only that she seemed to love the party life."

Chapter 24

Washington Shuffle

Mark took my arm, and we cut across Constitution Avenue in silence.

"Maybe something will happen now. I realize there is much more than a vaccine at stake for you," he said. "Blossom is at the core of much of what you're doing."

Surprised by his soft-spoken words, I felt my throat constrict. I nodded. "Timing is everything. Our luck at keeping Blossom alive is running out. I'm afraid people will forget—that she matters."

"I understand." He shook his head. "But ... we'll never know unless we try."

It was a hot day in Washington, DC, a city of beauty, elegance, sophistication, cherry blossoms, political maneuvering, lobbyists, and backroom deals. The town had it all, except for statehood. Tip: Use "District of Columbia" on address forms and for GPS navigation. A leisurely hour-long drive to the capitol from Mary's farm if you avoid the traffic snarls starting at six in the morning on I-66.

No kidding. Mary and I were born in an "asylum" on Massachusetts Avenue. The historic Columbia Hospital for Women and Lying-in Asylum was founded in 1866 and demolished by the time I got back to take a tour in 2002.

Mark had switched out his cameras and multi-pocketed vest for a dark blue casual jacket, slacks, crisp checkered shirt, and cushiony black shoes. His quick smile and lanky six-foot-three stature gave an overall impression of an easy-going, eclectic world traveler. The overstuffed, green canvas knapsack was a dead giveaway.

I dressed to blend with the sophisticated set. Within the hour, my feet throbbed, my blazer hung through the strap of my shoulder bag, and the humidity had coiled my strawberry-blond ponytail into ringlets.

Mark reached into his knapsack and handed me a cold bottle of water. *Cold? And, I didn't even think to bring a pair of sneakers?*

While I drank, he pulled a slim book out of his shirt pocket, jotted a note, then slipped it back. "Pardon me. Must have hundreds of these books. We're going to have a long day. But first, I want to thank you for your interest in SpayVac."

Shy with the compliment, I shrugged. "No problem."

"No, I mean it. For years I have made a case for humane wildlife birth control, with little support, and then you reached out.

"We'll get the updates on the Wild Horse and Burro Program and see if they've made headway for SpayVac in the Senate. The success of funding any federal program requires networking—building strong relationships and advocates."

"Wild horses and donkeys?"

He hesitated. "This is only one piece of the puzzle. Now it's about wild horses vs. the cattle industry and the lands controlled by the government. The recent public uproar over publicized helicopter round-ups and horse slaughter lit a fire. Now, we have the opportunity to prove our stuff. If SpayVac gains acceptance for wild horses, it will have vast implications for deer in urban communities across the country. My strategy is to go at this through the back door. We need public involvement.

"Politics doesn't smell of roses, does it? But there are some knowledgeable people out there trying to help."

I was getting a crash lesson in government bureaucracy. Our next stop was the US Department of the Interior.

"A friend of mine, Bud Cribley, is the Deputy Assistant Director of the Renewable Resources Division," he said. "Only a few blocks or so from here."

Or so? My feet were pounding.

There was nothing particularly "woodsy" about the offices, except for some Ansel Adams prints and a wildlife scene of jagged mountains, a winding stream, and an elk staring straight at someone's camera. Four identical chairs lined one wall, a nondescript couch, a couple of square end tables, a small bookcase, and a fake tree.

"Stark in here," I observed.

"You expected the Davy Crockett, 'king of the wild frontier' look, eh?" Mark grinned. "The government keeps things simple."

"A bit more country-rustic and a live plant or two wouldn't hurt."

Bud Cribley came into the room; hand extended in greeting. After introductions, his assistant joined us, carrying a pile of folders. He led the way into a side conference room where six cushioned leather chairs surrounded a pine table. Reference books, field reports, and a biography of John Muir, founder of the Sierra Club, were stacked on one side.

I could see the level of respect the two men shared—the wildlife scientist and the forestry expert. Bud had a rugged bearing about him: a strong jaw, deep-set eyes, and a broad smile under a thick mustache. He appeared more like an explorer than a government official, someone who would prefer to be hiking instead of sitting behind a desk managing the BLM's lands.

There was genuine excitement in his voice when he spoke of the projects on his agenda until the conversation turned to the wildlife contraception program. He reached for a report, flipped through the pages, then gestured to us.

"You would be surprised at how much the Bureau of Land Management spends on horse gathering and aftercare." Bud leaned back in the leather chair, which squeaked in protest. "The agency has the legal right to remove horses and burros to prevent deterioration of the ranges associated with overpopulation. There is a great need for easy contraception like SpayVac. You'll appreciate this." Bud swiveled a spreadsheet toward Mark. Mark quickly scanned it and traced his finger down the columns of data. "SpayVac was tested and proven." He moved his field note binders across the table to Bud. "This vaccine could ultimately save the government millions of dollars a year."

"We know." Bud opened both his hands on the table. "Remarkably, wasteful spending gets budgeted in. But, there's no money for a preventative to the problems we're facing. A mismatch."

"*Ahem*, we call them marketing specialists." Bud's assistant grimaced. "Seemingly, everything this country is doing now is paying for that horrible war in Iraq. They just voted to pull funding to study gun violence in this country, even though thirty-thousand Americans die each year.

"If we can hold on for another year, hopefully, the next president will present a different viewpoint, and research money gets allotted to a wildlife vaccine. I like guns. I just don't like bad people with guns," he said.

Mark tented his fingers under his chin. "What I'm afraid of is that SpayVac will be kept in limbo for years until the idea for a fertility control vaccine runs out of steam. Without money

for additional research or funds to meet the regulatory require-
ments, it's as good as over. SpayVac will not be available for
investigational use simply because no one will make it, despite
its efficacy and economic benefits."

"You're meeting with Senator Ron Wyden, from Oregon?
He's a good guy. He suggested that the Bureau of Land
Management make a positive lead statement to spearhead the
wildlife contraception effort. We're trying to involve more
groups to sign on. He wants to discuss your fieldwork."

Mark sighed and roused himself with what seemed to me
like weary resignation. He picked up the photograph of Blossom
and passed it to Bud. "No doubt, SpayVac needs the public to
act as its lobby. Wouldn't it be something if this doe could open
some hearts up on the hill?"

* * *

We cut across broad avenues, past pristine monuments, and
architecturally "serious" buildings on the way to the Senate
Office complex. The city was immaculate. Neoclassical buildings and monuments of white marble, most flying the stars and
stripes, some with touches of gold filigree, like swirls of icing
on a wedding cake. The six-hundred-foot-tall Washington
Monument towered over all.

I headed for a low stone seating wall separating the wide
sidewalk from one of the three buildings servicing US Senators
and their staffs. Stoicism gets you only so far. I needed to sit.
"I climbed the steps to the top of the Washington Monument
once in the '60s, but my leg muscles cramped. I took the elevator
down. Speaking of slowing down, let's rest a bit."

Mark let his knapsack slide to the stone ledge and reached
into it for more water and two snack bars. "I didn't realize how
heavy my field notebooks were.

"Would you look at that?" he said.

I followed his gaze across the street toward a configuration of possibly eight people walking in the shape of a triangular delta wing. Every one of them wore a dark suit.

"It's called a tactical guidance 'diamond' formation, used to protect dignitaries. That's something you don't witness every day."

"Reminds me of a group of migrating snow geese," I said.

The lead "bird" of the formation increased the pace as the group crossed the street. They synchronized within an arm's length of each other, headed in our direction, heralded by the *click, click, click* of a woman's heels. I shifted my attention to the pivotal leader: sensible heels amidst the group of men, the blond hair—the "wing" of protection—completed the picture of the new junior senator from New York, Hillary Rodham Clinton.

The group passed a few yards from us, intense faces scanning for whatever it is that bodyguards listen and watch for. Mark and I were the only people nearby. Apparently, we seemed reasonably benign—good citizen types. Senator Clinton glanced at us, saw that we recognized her, and without missing a beat, she grinned and winked. We watched the senator's security detail turn the corner of the building with drill team precision.

Rows of metal and glass doors opened into the uninspiring white marble lobby of the Hart Senate Office Building, as shiny and clean as a hospital vestibule, and just as inviting. We joined a group of people at a bank of elevators and squeezed in between several men, most with large briefcases. They stood, stiff and impressive in their silence, waiting to be released into the bustle of governmental routine.

The old elevator whirred and whined. Call it intuition, but when the lights flickered off and the elevator creaked to a halt between floors, I was not surprised.

The emergency lights blinked on, but not the recycling fan. Anxious men shuffled with no place to go. It got warm fast, and the air felt thick with sweat. Someone pried the bronze doors open a few inches, revealing a solid concrete wall, a blatant reminder that we were stuck in a tight, narrow shaft between floors.

Could we fall? Did jumping up before impact really work?

I saw a white-haired man near the rear wall struggle to loosen his tie. He pitched forward on the shoulder of another man, gasping for breath. Even in dim emergency lighting, his face looked flushed and sweaty.

"Give him room." I maneuvered toward him. "Are you diabetic?" I asked the man. "Anyone have anything sugary?" If he had too much sugar in his blood, sugar wouldn't help but also wouldn't hurt. But, if he had too much insulin, anything containing sugar could save his life. I took his arm and pulled him toward the front.

First, reassure the patient.

"I was a paramedic. I want you to lean up against the metal doors. You'll feel better. They're cold." Mark passed over a small container of juice.

"Thank you," the man said. He took two steps toward the bronze doors and flattened his hands and face against the cool surface. His breathing became less labored. He drank the juice and started to regain control. "Not diabetic." His chin fell slowly to his chest; he took a deep breath and closed his eyes.

There was pounding and a voice from above muffled within the walls of the elevator shaft. "Shut the doors!" Then, the slow whine of a motor and the elevator leveled to the floor above. The doors opened, and fresh air flooded the car. The shaken passengers spilled out into the hall.

"Senator, you all right?" A young man and woman hovered anxiously around the man I had helped. He leaned on the arm of a young staffer, turned back, and nodded to us. "Thank you," he said before walking away.

"Senator?" I asked Mark. "I wish I knew his name."

"Me too. Good job back there." He patted me on the arm and glanced at his watch.

"Thanks." I felt proud.

"In a few months, I've got to help with the 'gather' at the Wild Horse Sanctuary in California. You'd like those folks. You can help to give the SpayVac injections to the mares. Why not?" He smiled. "You have skills."

Mark picked up the pace through rose-colored marble floor corridors lined on either side by solid mahogany doors and brass plaques engraved with the who's who of senatorial movers and shakers.

United States Senator Ron Wyden of Oregon.

"I'm sorry. Senator Wyden is on his way to the Senate floor for a vote." Mandy, a young staffer, indicated the closed-circuit TV monitor summoning Senators to cast their votes on a piece of legislation.

She continued, "He wanted me to relay his thoughts on the route to get quick money to SpayVac. It involves getting it earmarked, setting aside funds, on legislation. He wants you to know that he's in the loop. He'll sign on and is having ongoing talks with the Oregon Equine Practitioners and members of Congress to spearhead the effort. I'm sorry you missed him."

Mark was reflective on the drive back to Mary's farm in The Plains.

"I recognize that the most we can hope for is an 'eartag' on a piece of legislation." He reached over and tapped my hand. "Just another first step." He looked grim. "I'll follow up tomorrow."

Always tomorrow.

Blossom would give birth to another baby soon, and then, the year after that, if she lived, would have another one or two.

Most would be killed for sport within thirty-six months.

Chapter 25

Storm Front

New Jersey was in for a monster storm. Rain-driven thunder-heads churned across the sky, followed by bands of humid, dead calm air. An intermittent horn-alarm signaled another weather alert on the office TV.

BREAKING NEWS! ...
BE PREPARED TO TAKE ACTION!

Thunderstorms are expected to continue across the northern New Jersey area. Grounds remain saturated. Six inches of more heavy rainfall raises the potential of flash flooding. FLASH FLOODING IS A VERY DANGEROUS SITUATION. There is often little lead-time.

I stepped through the leg straps of the ankle length rain-coat I used for trail riding, zipped up, and pulled the hood over my baseball cap. "I'll feed the animals, then take another look around. Heaven forbid Blossom has her baby today."

"Check your watch," Pino didn't hesitate. "Won't take me more than a half-hour to hook up the generator. I'll hurry."

Bracing against wind blasts threatening to turn each step into a slide, I sloshed toward the alpaca shed. I paused, stared up, transfixed by the roaring, twisting canopy of poplars, thrashing and slapping each other, like kickboxers in a cage.

Off-road tire-boots would help.

The hum of alpaca-talk, mixed with squeaky-toy sounds from a few nervous youngsters, filled the space as they huddled in tight groups. Both waterers were full. I added some alfalfa treats to the feed bins. "Sorry, kids, no time to play. Hi, and goodbye."

I latched the door behind me, checked my watch, then veered toward the high ground on the north side of the horse barn. Twenty minutes left to my half-hour check-in with Pino.

The aroma of clean horses, fresh wood shavings, and new hay pleased me, as much as the bouquet of purple lilacs on the kitchen table did at breakfast. Justinian nickered and stretched his head over the stall guard, into the aisle. He fidgeted and grumbled with anxiety. I fussed with his forelock, tickled his chin, and tossed a fresh ear of corn in his bin.

Across the aisle, Simba was stretched out on cushiony-soft pine bark bedding, and Protto Call munched hay contentedly from his wall rack. Poncho and Sparky, the minis, shared a stall and started vying for the expected goodies in my pocket. Nothing ever rocks those two.

If we lost electricity, we'd lose well water. Before closing the barn doors, I topped off four extra water buckets, hung a low-light lantern in the aisle, and tossed apples in each of the feed bins.

"Blossom!" My voice went nowhere in the wind. Pinpoint rain-drops stung and clicked like buckshot on my raincoat. I hurried to the side gates and along the fence line, where I saw her last.

She's close. I feel it.

Can intuition be words? I sensed a pull as if the words had been spoken.

Here.

Inexplicably, where to search became clear.

Bent against the storm, I made my way to an overgrown area between the shed and knee-high rock wall bordering Rose Cottage. The earth smelled mossy, felt slimy, and the footing was deep in rot, except around old trees, where seasoned roots could be used for balance. A sodden hedgerow of lilacs sagged against the stones to the street. I would loop back toward the house from there.

What if a snake is hiding in this muck, or worse, a family of snakes? What if Faccia-brutta, the snake, and his missus show up? With the kids?

The idea was scary but struck me as funny.

From the West, Mother Nature's boom box blasted. Thunder- clouds swelled and banged their way across the ground—coming closer, like a rowdy caravan of gypsy tinkers. I counted the time between flashes and claps of thunder to deter-mine the distance to the storm in miles.

One thousand one, one thousand two, one thousand three.

As if a switch had been flipped, the rain was gone, replaced by a thick humid air mass—everything hushed, with not even the croak of a frog to break the eerie stillness. I took off my cap and let my raincoat hang open.

"*Aehh ...*"

She was under the hedge! With a surge of relief, I pushed aside the flower-drenched branches and squinted into the dim light.

"Blossom?"

With an effort, she shifted her head from the fawn cuddled tightly against her, nose-nudged my hand, and gazed at me with a soulful stare. She appeared exhausted, worn out, and worried.

The thought of losing her frightened me. "I'm here my girl."

"Anna!" Pino was coming toward me in a defensive crouch, yelling words that were smothered by the storm.

"She's under the hedge!" I stood as spidery cloud-to-cloud lightning split the gunmetal sky, turning it black. A weird prickling sensation crossed my scalp.

"She had the baby."

"GET DOWN! Your hair is standing straight up!"

Terrifying hissing noises began, and all the leaves—on every tree and every bush—shivered in the electrical charge. Unusual pops and clicks seemed to radiate from the ground.

With a sob, I crouched and covered my head with my hands. The atmosphere sizzled, as if it were on fire, claw-like streaks of lightning ripped across the sky, and exploded in a horrendous display of power.

CRRAACK!

My body rebounded from the electrostatic ground punch. Waves of thunder rumbled for half a minute or more.

"We got lucky. If you can call that luck." Pino lifted me by my arms. "Lightning hit the sub-station tower on Fox Hill. I saw it."

"I'm okay—I think."

A pungent odor of ozone permeated everything. "Smell that? The air smells of burnt wiring."

"*Neahhh* ..." The fawn squealed. "My God. Blossom! The baby!"

The dark space under the hedge was now full of gentle, little noises: Blossom's licks to her baby's face, the fawn's hiccups, drops of water trickling along leafy channels, drip-dripping to the ground.

"Let's get them to the house," Pino said, lifting the fawn from her. Bundled under his jacket so that only its four pointy feet stuck out, he started for home.

Blossom tried to follow, but fell back, too weak to roll to her knees. She closed her eyes.

My fingers probed for a pain response, pressed the bones of her skull, swooped over her spine, the milk-filled udder, her butt, to the tip of her tail. *Huh?* My eyes jerked to her tail, trying to make sense of the now stubby end, inches shorter, its white-haired tip was gone. I leaned closer. The hair was cut neatly as if blunted with scissors. Clean—no blood—cut?

I shifted my position to pull her forward, then stopped at the sight of a tiny, stillborn fawn behind her, tucked between the dark, shrubby root crowns. She had given birth to twins.

"Aw—" I sat back on my heels.

Pino returned with a bath towel. "How's she doing?" I pointed to the stillborn fawn. "Look."

"Maybe that's why she didn't want to leave."

"It's more than that. The tip of her tail is gone."

"What do you mean?"

"Exactly that. Gone. Cut off. And, look at her. She looks drugged."

We worked the towel into a makeshift sling. "Lift with your legs," Pino reminded.

"Do we have any Cheerios left? She loves Cheerios," I said.

★ ★ ★

The lazy stream bordering Unicorn Hollow exploded into a raging current, and the rain softened to a heavy drizzle. The lower paddocks continued to flood, crashing branches, poles, and horse jumps into the narrow bridge crossing underneath Fox Hill Road.

I handed the binoculars to Pino.

"What a clean-up job we're going to have," he said. "You said we were running low on firewood, right?"

We shuffled in and out of the kitchen, ate a quick dinner, and watched the after-effects of the storm. Blossom had eaten a bowl of Cheerios, horse chow, and blueberries, groomed her fawn, went outside to take care of "business," and came back.

Within minutes she was sleeping peacefully with her baby on her old bed in the kitchen. Kaya was with them.

It would be a long night.

The events of the previous day churned into a soupy mix of drama and nagging questions. Shortly, before 5:00 a.m., I dressed. The house was still dark, with only a nightlight in the foyer and a flashing red message light from the answering machine on my kitchen desk.

I pushed the play button.

"H-hello, Anna ..." The caller cleared his throat in a nervous, whiny giggle. "Did your deer survive the storm? You owe me for letting her live ..."

I imagined his pathetic smirk and replayed the words through clenched teeth. Background sounds on the tape hummed while I waited, and winced at the disconnecting click—fear in my veins. I leaned against the wall, but this time did not cry.

I'll find a way to get you.

"Aehh ..." Blossom peeked around the center island cabinet. She was alert, her old self. I nuzzled the fur on the back of her neck.

"Neahhh ..." *Clickity, clickity, crash, bang.* Long-legged

awkwardness landed the fawn under his mother. He scrambled to his feet, bumping her, me, the cabinets, and boldly glancing around—a young cowboy with a touch of swagger. No doubt, his father's side of the family.

"You're a real Buckaroo." The name fit.

I sat on the floor and let the fawn come to me.

I needed some balance, time to think things through. I plugged in the tea kettle, set out two cups, and went to wake Pino.

THE LANGUAGE OF ANIMALS

"How can you tell," the child asked,
"What animals want to say?"
"They tell me," his mother said,
"When they visit me each day."

"Mother, I do not understand this thing
You do without words to share."
"Let your mind be still my child, and
They will know how much you care."

The child looked with innocent eyes
At creatures with no human voice,
And listened with an awakened heart
To learn there really is a choice to

Reach beyond mere human thoughts, and
See the world in a different way.
Animal voices have their meaning
In how they grieve and how they play; so

children, look into animal eyes, and
Their words will come like rain.
You'll see the beauty of their thoughts.
You'll see their love and share their pain.

— JEANNE HAMILTON TROAST

Chapter 26

Second Chances

The temperature rose with the summer sun. Another brutal weather front walloped the already waterlogged countryside the night before, and raging streams created mud bogs that could have torn a horse's leg tendons to shreds. A good day to stay home.

After his bubble bath, Justinian felt soft as a rabbit and smelled aromatic, like a sachet ball of citrus peel. For more than an hour, I had scrubbed and groomed my horse until he shone like a pearl. It was worth it. He nickered his contentment and brushed his sensitive muzzle across my back.

I heard the grinding squeak from the wooden gates to Unicorn Hollow, a rustic alarm of sorts. I unsnapped Justinian's halter, tapped his rump, and watched him take off. Near the house, he stopped, went down on his knees, and rolled. Dirty again, but happy.

A car was parked next to the entrance, and a frantic young man waved his arms to get my attention. He bumped the gate open with his backside. The girl behind him struggled under the weight of an unusually large fawn, cradling its head beneath her chin, its long legs bumping against the girl's shins as she hurried to the barn. They were soaking wet.

"Ahorramos el venado," the boy said, out of breath. *We save the deer.* "Are you Missus Anna? Johnson people, on Homestead Farm, say you will help us. We know of Blossom." He clasped his fists to his chest and gestured toward the girl.

"This is Amparo, my sister. I am Jose."

The girl struggled to lower the fawn gently to the ground. Her waist-length, black hair clung, like seaweed, over the fawn's body and her smooth copper skin and shirt.

"Pobrecito," she purred. *Poor little thing.* She slid her hands under its shoulders and rocked its head and chest on her lap. Amparo lifted her face with full, half-hopeful eyes.

"No muerto, mira," she said.

"*Not dead, look*," Jose translated.

I pushed the hair back from her face and wiped the girl's tear-streaked cheeks with my fingertips. "Amparo, let me see. It will be okay."

Jose explained. "Amparo see baby in stream, stuck in bush. We hold hands. Go in together to save." Jose twisted his arms in a tumbling motion to lend credence to the water rescue.

The fawn breathed in crisp snaps, like a bag of popcorn cooking on a hot stove. I realized the struggle the fawn must have endured, and how heroic this young boy and girl were to battle the harsh floodwaters to save it.

"Por favor, Amparo." We lifted the fawn from her, as one would handle a fragile piece of porcelain. I had seen near drownings before. Bracing the fawn's body in my arms, I swung him, head down in an arc, like the pendulum of a grandfather clock, then thumped along his back to help expel anything he might have inhaled from the stream.

His mouth strained open to gag, but only a small amount of water dripped out. Pneumonia would be a possibility soon, and I had no antibiotics. "Quick ... come." I turned into the barn. "Come with me."

Protocols of emergency techniques for animals buzzed around in my mind. A virtual stew of life-saving actions, as haphazard as any recipe calling for "a little bit of this, and a little piece of that." A conglomeration of ideas learned as a paramedic or realized through my experiences on the farm.

Pino and I had received our Rabies vaccine booster, a life-saving precaution for anyone dealing with animals daily. There is no cure for Rabies. "Get vaccinated," I always tell everyone. Never take a chance.

I spoke in halting Spanish. "Amparo, cuide al bebe." *Watch the baby.*

"Jose, drag the straw to the wash stall, por favor."

I covered the bale with a clean saddle pad and flipped the switch to the ceiling-mounted infrared heat lamp. A bunched-up towel under the fawn's bottom maintained its head-down position. Medical supplies had been organized, and stored in the tack room cabinet, ready for an emergency.

The fawn's gums looked pale, his pulses weak, eyes reactive but sluggish. He didn't budge when the large-bore needle pierced his belly skin, and I pushed 50cc's of replacement fluids into his abdomen. Amparo closed her eyes and leaned heavily against her brother. Jose sat her down on the tack trunk in the aisle.

It had been quite a while since any animal needed critical care on the farm. The baby deer jerked his head away when I snugged the two-pronged nasal oxygen cannula in his nostrils and secured the tubing behind his soft, furry ears.

"Sorry, little one," I murmured.

I forgot to lower the volume on my electronic stethoscope. It blasted a crackle of fluid and an erratic heartbeat into my head, as loud as any on-stage amplifier. "*Eeech*!" I yanked the plugs out of my ears.

Jose grinned.

The fawn made a weak effort to stretch, and another round of spasms racked his body. Whimpering, he flopped his head from side to side. The oxygen flowed steadily, but if his lungs were clogged ... To push more blood to his heart and maintain blood pressure, I squeezed his ankles in an upward, reverse milking-like technique.

He was a strong boy, had been cared for and nurtured, and was at least six weeks old.

"*Neahhh ...*"

"Hang in there, baby." I turned him, continually thumping his chest. One minute ... two minutes. Still, a heart out of sync and contaminated lungs struggling for air. I sat back on my heels and mentally scrambled for a solution to halt the downward spiral of inevitable shock. Every guttural sound from his chest was another reminder.

"Aw, Missus," Amparo mumbled. Jose stood quietly against the wood plank wall.

Now what?

The oxygen level indicator on the tank showed three-quarters full. I transferred the nasal cannula to my nose and secured the loop of tubing behind my ears, turned up the air flow valve, wedged my index finger into the fawn's mouth, positioned his head to straighten his neck, and breathed—one—two—three deep hyperventilating inhalations. I held the last breath, covered the fawn's mouth and nose with my mouth, and puffed the enriched air gently into his lungs.

"*Phuuhh ... phuuhh ... phuuhh.*"

My hand rode his expanding chest with each breath I pushed into him, then applied steady downward pressure to his ribcage. I waited for the air to return against my cheek. Another two inhalations of oxygen-enriched air restarted the cycle—back and forth, from airway to lungs—a mesmerizing, integrated rhythm of gentle compressions.

My breath became his breath; my hand became his lungs. "Amparo, look, Blossom!" Jose said.

Blossom had come into the barn and stood next to me without so much as a lick to my hand.

The fawn made a spastic effort toward Blossom, as he would have undoubtedly reached for the security of his mother. He jerked his legs under him and, for a few seconds, wobbled his head upright.

"*Aehhh* ..." Without hesitating, she shoved her nose under his belly, trying to flip him over, as she did with her own fawns. Amparo gasped and reached to push her away.

"No, no, it's okay," I cautioned and restrained her with a gentle touch to her arm.

Blossom nudged him again. "*Aehhh* ..." She kept on, bumping and stimulating him, piercing the lethargy that threatened to shut down his body.

"Blossom, easy ... not so rough." She licked the fawn's eyes and ears, sniffed at his mouth, forcing it open. He coughed and choked up a wad of grass and what could have been a small twig. I wiped it away with a cloth.

"Open wide," I said. Secure on my lap, I aimed my flashlight into his mouth, expecting to see a red, bruised throat. Instead, I found a glob of stringy debris jammed into his soft back palate, disappearing down his throat.

"Whew," I sighed, releasing my grip and allowing him to calm down before starting again. "You must have swallowed the stream, baby."

Using the fawn's gag reflexes in a give and take effort reminded me of working a too-big fish at the end of a lightweight fishing line. I tugged and thumped his sides with a cupped hand and released what I hoped was the complete obstruction from his airway.

"*Neahhh* ..." he squeaked.

"All gone," I murmured, rocking the weak baby. I repositioned the oxygen tubing near his nose and gently placed him on a thick horse blanket. He looked around, took another deep breath, and finally rested.

"Where is Blossom?" I asked.

"She take apple from bucket." Jose smiled. "Then go out." I grinned at Amparo. "Le salvaste la vida." *You saved his life.*

"Si." She clapped her hands wildly over her head and twirled, as excited as any young girl could get.

★ ★ ★

The paddocks finally dried out, but a musky aroma hovered over the smorgasbord of cedar and cypress branches, mixed with manure and muck.

It was a hard time for the orphaned fawn we now called Baby Boomer. He vied desperately for Blossom's attention, shoving Buckaroo aside, maneuvering under Blossom to fight for milk, and generally annoying the heck out of her.

"Mark told me our local deer would reject him because he's from another herd. But Blossom? I don't understand why she doesn't like him," I said. "It's totally out of character."

"Keep the faith," Pino said. "She's not exactly like most deer." And so, we waited. Occasionally, Blossom showed curiosity, giving the fawn a sniff and a lick, but without much promise.

He was not hers.

We had to do something.

Several mornings later, Baby Boomer walked out of the front door with Pino, Kaya, and me. A healthy, full-bellied little guy—full of resilience and high spirits—his white tail straight up. He jumped from the foyer over the three stone steps to the blue stone, turned, and waited for us to follow—a happy sight.

Blossom, baby Buckaroo, and three other deer were grazing near the road. Blossom started toward us, saw Boomer, and stopped.

"Wonder what she's waiting for," Pino said.

I watched her take another step forward, pause, then step back.

"She's trying to decide between him and us."

If she turns away, we've lost her confidence.

Still, something held her back until finally, she made up her mind—and walked—toward us.

Chapter 27

Baby Boomer

B aby Boomer had it all. Poise, pizzazz, good looks, and a streak of stubbornness that wouldn't let up. How could I not compare them?

Blossom was the total girly package: sweet, sleek, and diminutive, with light tawny coloring and a cutesy demeanor.

She belonged in pink. Boomer was boyishly cute, stocky, and robust, with chunky cheeks, intense brown-black eyes, and swirls of hair hiding nubby antler buds. His neck was muscular and set high on his shoulders, giving him an aura of aloofness, especially evident compared to the other fawns.

I should have called him Sherlock. He investigated everything, from the apple he rolled with his nose and the flower he snuffled, to the friends he played with and the tree he lazed under. Much of the time, his nose sniffed skyward, trying to coax the truth out of some smell wafting by.

Oh, how it all came together when he moved. I don't even have to shut my eyes to remember the way his neck arched, his young chest expanded, how his knee raised, toe pointed, in one flawless movement—a perfect miniature of the impressive buck he would become.

A floral blast of golden-coned Echinacea drew butterflies and a variety of bees to our lively garden. Pino and I spent the morning trimming wisteria vines and shrubbery from fencing near the pool. At noon I was meeting Jeanne and Ellie at the General Store.

"My bird!" Caruso screeched from close behind me. I jumped.

Caruso, "my bird" as he referred to himself, fluffed his wings, spread his rainbow-colored tail feathers, and swaggered toward me along the top of the six-foot-high fence. He stretched his neck, an accordion of green and yellow feathers, while singing his version of an opera by, dare I say, Puccini?

Typical of yellow-naped Amazon parrots, Caruso cocked his head sideways, one amber-colored eye scanning the sky, ready to pivot into a tail-up stance if a predator hawk soared too close. Shaggy, eight-pound Kaya woofed at Caruso, on guard for any hint that he'd jump down and run after her. We all knew the wrath of the "green varmint" and high-stepped away from the ever-ready beak of "my bird."

Sweet Pea, Claire, her twin fawns, and little Buckaroo grazed across the road, while Blossom lazed in her favorite spot under the Acer maple, observing Boomer play catch and release with a particularly leafy branch. We all paused to watch him stand on his hind legs, hooking his front feet over the branch before letting it snap back with a swoosh.

"Climbing trees now, Boomer?" I pocketed my clippers and went over.

Slender blades of grass dangled from Blossom's mouth. She could get a lot out of a mouthful of food. Eat—swallow—regurgitate it up again as cud—chew it again. The same meal would always be the next meal.

The mechanics of effective eating were all about anatomical precision. A deer's powerful jaw muscles and molars can easily crush a corn cob within seconds. And yet, nip succulent leaves cleanly with front lower teeth against a bony upper pad. To me, the most surprising and extraordinary eating structure in Blossom's mouth was a thin, flattish spine of inconspicuous serrated skin bordering her inner lips, which sliced through leaves as neatly as a razor blade.

Suddenly, the cry of an angry blue jay tore through the greenery. Feathery-blue, white, and fierce, it squawked and flapped against Boomer's head, smacking him with its wings and claws, pecking at his nose in a bold effort to protect its nest.

Boomer scrambled, fell, and ended up straddling Blossom's back.

Annoyed, Blossom stood and shook him off. The young buck slid under her belly and swiftly rolled to his knees, and without skipping a beat, his mouth reached for her udder. Blossom had had it. She lifted her back leg and shoved him over, pinning him with her foreleg.

"Whew, he never gives up."

"He's becoming too much for her," Pino said. We were getting used to his roughhousing, but there were times when Blossom's eyes were puffy from lack of rest and from dealing with her baby, let alone this orphaned youngster who never slowed down. I had been privy to her child-rearing techniques with her previous fawns. Blossom was a strict disciplinarian and would not be a pushover as a surrogate mother to Boomer.

"*Neahhh* ..." Boomer squirmed and ducked.

It seemed to us that Blossom aggressively groomed him until he calmed down, rewarding him by shortening the time she spent cleaning his already cleaned ears. We waited for the inevitable.

"Time for a long and thorough ear-licking," Pino said.

"He's getting better at listening, don't you think?" I said.

★ ★ ★

Darn it! Jeanne and Ellie were probably at The General Store by now, and I was already ten minutes late when I turned out of our driveway and headed to town. Halfway down Fox Hill, a maroon pickup eased behind me, tailgating, honking, and goading me to drive faster until the turnoff to Oldwick.

What's your problem, buddy?

In the rearview mirror, I saw the driver's hand slap against the door, as if following a beat or in annoyance. I tapped my breaks and eased my car to the side of the road. He passed, hand now raised, middle finger up, signaling his big win.

Jerk.

I parked at the rear of the building and hurried up weathered brick steps to the restaurant. From across the room, Ellie waved and walked over.

"Sorry, I'm late." I gave her an enthusiastic hug.

"No problem. Jeanne's holding an outside table for us."

"Hiya, gals." Al greeted us from behind the takeout counter.

"You'd better grab the last quiche—just came out of the oven. Comes with raspberry brandy puree. Anna, go, get a look at Blossom's poster. It's taking on a life of its own." He smiled.

Blossom's poster had dominated the community bulletin board for the past three years, but someone, probably Al, recently stapled a plastic daisy and pen on a string to one corner. Hearts, smiley faces, signatures of well-wishers, prayers, and even a cutout paper rainbow said it as well as the words: "Can't wait to see you" ... "Love you" ... and, my favorite, printed in a child's scrawl, "Don't worry. No one will ever shoot you. They promised. Your best friends, Richie, Jan & Billy Boy."

At the garden table, the conversation and mood got serious, fast.

"So, give us the details. It makes absolutely no sense to ... what did you call it on the phone? ... collect the hair from a deer tail?" Jeanne asked. "Unless—"

"Unless what?" I asked. "What else could it mean?" I paused, remembering. "Blossom could hardly hold her head up. Makes no sense to me, either. The white tip of her tail was squared-off a half inch or so beyond the end of her tailbone. No blood, nothing like that. He must have drugged her."

"But you can't be sure," Ellie said, cutting into a slice of still warm quiche. She took a bite. "*Mmm* ... Al's right. Try it with the raspberry sauce."

Jeanne leaned closer and considered for a moment. "Could be ... suppose he has something like a fetish. People talk about the spirit of deer. About their tails being charms, as antennas to the Almighty. It's stupid to leave a voice message, though. Easy enough to play the bully from a safe distance."

"A no-brainer." Ellie shook her head. "Let's just say he's doing it—because he can. He's watching you. That makes him a stalker. Although, I think he would have done it by now if he wanted to."

"Done what?" I asked.

Her voice faltered. "Killed her."

I winced.

"That's all I think about now," I said. "How to stop him, or anyone else, planning to kill her." I gulped the tart lemonade.

Jeanne tilted her head back in her chair and stared into the sky. "I completely agree. This isn't a joke. I hate this guy, who-ever he is. Did Pino ever speak to him?"

"No," I said. "He would have, but whenever he answers the phone, the caller hangs up. So, there's no telling for sure."

"Lower your voices," Ellie whispered. "We're upsetting the guy at the next table. He's been eavesdropping since we sat down."

"Who?" I turned into the penetrating gaze of a stocky mid-dle-aged man with brushes for eyebrows. His eyes narrowed, red splotches crept over his neck and face, and a toothpick upped its pace between his lips. If first impressions counted, this man needed a good scrubbing.

He stood, causing the metal chair to scrape across the bricks, cocked a finger in my direction, and left. The words, "God said: The Earth and Everything Else is Mine," were printed on his black tee.

I rolled my shoulders to relieve the tension, took a deep breath. "I can't stand it. I'm fed up with these people. See that? He's angry—and, for what? Because I'm friends with a deer—a wild animal with more character than he has in his little finger?"

"*Shhh* ... don't," Jeanne said quietly.

"Horrible man, thankfully, he's going." Ellie put her hand on top of mine. She gulped lemonade. "Too bad this isn't a gin and tonic."

Before they left, I looked into the caring faces of my friends. "Guess I've lost my giggles. Sorry."

Twenty minutes later, he was still there, between the news-paper rack and the front door, stalled at Blossom's poster. He glanced up, more curious than surprised.

As close to nonchalant as I could muster, I opened my mouth to say something smart and choked. I had no plan, and the words wouldn't come. I turned to leave, saw Al watching from across the room, and then stopped.

Do it. Do it now!

I walked over to him. "Nice shirt." I remained motionless, using prissy words to break the ice. Nervous under his gaze, I nodded at the picture. "We're asking people to save her life ... by not shooting."

Silence.

"Just this one deer—she's my friend." I pointed to his shirt and tried to joke. "Hey. You can still own the rest of the earth."

He fidgeted with a small box on his keyring. "What I do is my business." His finger pointed close to my face. He spoke in a voice so low I could hardly hear. "And my business is none of yours."

My sensible side urged me to stop. I could not. Through clenched teeth, each word measured and full of disdain, I retorted, "You can count on it becoming my business if you ever touch her."

He turned, kicked open the door with one high-heeled cowboy boot, and sauntered out. The old wooden-framed screen door hung up a little before its fat spring recoiled, shimmied, and slammed shut behind him.

Shaken, I went back to the cozy confines of the gourmet coffee aisle.

"You can come out now." Al walked over, wiping his hands on a clean towel. "He's a weird one. Hope his pickup gets ticketed."

"A maroon pickup?" He nodded. "Why?"

Chapter 28

The Wild Ambassador of Tewksbury

I triangulated all the usual places. From Blossom's den to the slick granite outcropping, to the southernmost stream on our property. No signs of Blossom or Boomer. I divvied up a bunch of carrots between the horses and started their round pen training.

On cue, a dozen loud, goofy-looking guinea hens swooped down from the trees to gawk. Clucking and squawking, the gregarious bunch settled, fluffed, and preened their feathers within the four tubular metal rails, like live-action notes on a sheet of music.

It was a short workout—too much noise.

Tewksbury's tree trimmers were high in the canopy of oaks bordering Unicorn Hollow. Brawny, hard-hatted arborists in aerial lift buckets revved their chainsaws, took aim, and sliced through branches the utility company labeled "hazardous." The operator rotated the hydraulic extension arm down to its platform and climbed out of the bucket.

I walked over to him. "How do you stand the noise?"

He pointed to his bright orange ear protection. "Earmuffs. I'm also getting good at lip reading." He flashed a broad smile. "Say, how are your deer? Coolest thing. If they didn't wear those collars, I'd swear they were statues."

"You saw them?"

"About six this morning," he said. "The buck was standing; Blossom was lying by your front steps. They headed toward your neighbor's house when we cranked up the saws." He gestured toward our neighbor's pink bungalow. "Too much of a racket for them, I guess."

Giddy with relief, I hugged him.

"That was easy," he grinned. "I put the work order in your mailbox." He frowned. "Now, that doe ... she touches your heart. Hate to see her looking so thin. She sick?"

"Yeah." I felt the lump start in my throat.

"Our crew has been telling people about her for years. We call her the Wild Ambassador of Tewksbury. She's got quite a reputation. I even have a few pictures of her and the guys. She's a rarity. Who's the buck with the collar?"

"Baby Boomer."

"Boomer, huh? I'll address him by name next time." He took a few steps toward the truck, climbed on the running board, and tipped his hardhat. "Nice to actually meet you." He signaled the driver to go. With a series of beeps and the crunch of gravel, the trucks moved down the road.

Later that evening, I added the Work Order Form from the power company to Blossom's scrapbook. The signed, handwritten note in the "comments" section read:

"This in mailbox b'cuz I didn't want to disturb the family deer. Blossom and a buck relaxing by front door. Any questions call..."

★ ★ ★

Blossom was sick. Agonizingly sick. One morning, I found her curled tightly into herself beneath our bedroom window.

Within a month she lost a quarter of her body weight, shuffled with painful uncoordinated movements, and frequently had trouble getting up after she fell. Her tawny coat degraded into brittle, translucent fibers, raised needle-like straight up in her body's useless effort to control the raging fever.

Pleading for help within the veterinary community produced nothing.

"Please. She's hypersensitive to noise, touch, and especially light. It makes her squirm almost to the point of hysteria. She falls asleep in puddles on the side of the road, trying to cool off."

Regardless of the cause of her illness, her weakened body and unrelenting fever demanded an antibiotic. Most vets were sympathetic, but others didn't return my calls. It was against the law to help a deer, so it was no use trying to hide my frustration. I chided myself for assuming a vet would try to make humanitarian animal laws work for Blossom. In the end, she was "only" a wild deer.

"You know I can't," Dr. Shari said kindly. She, too, had seen battle with cancer and come back swinging into the competitive world of large animal veterinary medicine. Dr. Shari had the smarts, common sense, and gumption I hoped would help. And, she liked Blossom, a lot.

"Could Blossom have been poisoned?" she had asked.

Several members of Friends of Deer thought her symptoms suggested poisoning, using a common organic phosphate pesticide disguised in food. Ingested, a little at a time would have a cumulative effect. Blossom would die, slowly. One girl thought she was targeted because we were shaking up the hunting community. Another thought that "some people are just that way."

I was foggy-minded, yet coiled like a spring, unable to shut out the gnawing fear dragging me every place else but to sleep. Through half-closed eyes, I imagined the gauzy window sheers puffing into the bedroom as sails billowing on a calm sea—that didn't work. Tried to psyche myself into the illusion of the perfect day to come, with mellow wood notes and beautiful aromas wafting gently above lavender meadows. That didn't work either.

Pretending got me nowhere this time. Today would be another day spent searching for Blossom in places where I dreaded to look.

The past few days had started out unusually chilly and damp but warmed to the mid-70s by early afternoon. Without waking Pino, I finally rolled out of bed, slipped into flip-flops and my quilted robe, and snugged its belt into a bow. For one refreshing moment, its silky coziness added a much-needed dose of serenity.

To Blossom, the sun had become a debilitating enemy to hide from. Before the first rays spiked above the horizon and stung her swollen eyes, she would hide somewhere dark that promised relief.

Like navigating a rocky coastline without a map, I was doctoring her with intuition and a smattering of practical knowledge. To save time, I packed my knapsack with the pocket flashlight and safety whistle I always carried on the trail, syringes of Vitamin B12 and Banamine, a potent analgesic with anti-inflammatory properties, kept on hand for farm animal emergencies. An insulated section held a small bag of granola, blackberries, and a thermos mug for milk. I eased the strap over my shoulder and stepped outside.

I gasped in surprise. A white plastic bag had been taped to the brass door knocker, with a note. "A wish for Blossom— From your Fairy Godmother." An overwhelming sense of gratitude and hope washed over me. Protected within a rolled tube of cardboard and bubble wrap was a small vial and the words "broad-spectrum antibiotic."

The heavy mahogany door clicked shut behind me.

I heard her labored breathing before she emerged from the shadowy ornamental grasses edging the circular driveway. In the flat, pre-dawn dimness, where shadows were kind, her eyes bulged, and her body still appeared emaciated and skeletal.

"Blossom," I called softly, descended the steps, and knelt beside her.

"*Aehhh* ..." She stiffly drew her nose across my face in greeting. Perhaps today would be a turnaround day—the antibiotic offered another chance of success. It was the thirteenth day since starting my own injections for her. Thirteen times, I had rested my hands on her shoulders and bowed between her droopy ears with a kiss and a prayer.

Be safe.

Nagging, grim questions pinwheeled in my mind. Why weren't any of the other deer sick? Boomer, bonded as a shadow to Blossom over the past year, would have been susceptible to whatever malady she suffered.

Of course she was a target; there was a motive—a helpless, trophy deer trapped as a consequence of her personality.

The sun would be up soon. We were running out of time.

"*Wheee* ..." I faked a giggle and traced my fingers down her ribs into the sunken hollow of her stomach.

She liked that.

"Okay, girlie, let's get started." I measured out the antibiotic. "You ready for your meds? This one is a present from your Fairy Godmother. Must be magic." While probing for less sore spots in her muscles, I kept the chit-chat going. I hadn't forgotten how to give a good injection.

"Lucky for you, I have great technique." Next, a thick, cool washcloth for a compress across her head and eyes.

"*Aehhh* ..." She pushed into the cloth.

I held her face between my hands, my thumbs on the pressure points between her eyes, and squeezed. "One-two-three, pain go'way," I counted to her, releasing the pressure as she relaxed her head on my lap. I waited until she lifted her nose into the washcloth again, asking for more. "One-two-three, pain go'way," for as long as she wanted.

I know for a fact, my makeshift attempt at pain relief worked on my son Glen when he suffered from headaches as a child. "Mommy, the pain's all gone," he'd said in childish awe, as if he thought I really had hands that could heal.

"Guess what, Blossom?" I made a bowl of my hands and rocked them back and forth.

"Your tummy is just like a little round life raft caught between the waves in a rough sea." Her syrupy eyes swiveled toward me as if refocusing from within another dimension.

She was tolerating the daily injections well. Nowadays, with sharper, disposable needles, giving a good injection is much easier. And yet, even the best equipment in the wrong hands could ruin your day. I've seen it happen.

I'll never lose those memories of the kids' ward at St. Albans General or the pungent odors of alcohol and ointments from the medications cart that aides pushed down the hospital aisle twice a day. I can still hear the clunky rubber wheels on the super-shiny linoleum, sounding halfway between a squish and a squeak, effectively turning any happy "on" switches to "off." I think I can speak for every patient, all forty of us "ward kids," who cringed at the mandatory injections—hiding never worked for long.

It was an ominous sign if the "shot cart" was guided by anyone but my favorite, Nurse Kune. She'd get a shot into you as fast as my old cowboy hero Gene Autry drew the six-shooter from his holster.

One night, I volunteered to go first with a newbie nurse's aide. I was reluctant but willed myself to go forward, bravely offering my sacrificial right arm, swollen, black, blue, yellow, and green, like a thunderstorm with the sun behind it. I had an edge, so to speak because, after so much time in the ward, my arm was numb, but they didn't know.

The way she twisted the needle, I knew right away it was going to snap. I should have taken bets. The aide groaned and said, "Sorry." Some of the kids made wide rolling-eye signals of support from the sidelines.

No doubt, I upped my status. Little Viola, who had fallen headfirst into a bucket of hot tar eight months before, said her face and my arm looked "kinda like twins."

Soon, Nurse Kune was at my bedside, using tweezers to remove the needle from my arm. She was afraid my arm would become infected. She made a note on my chart not to allow me to "bamboozle" the aides into using my right arm again.

"But, Miss Kune, how come your shots don't hurt?"

Her eyebrows raised, and she leaned in with a conspiratorial whisper. "I'm Wonder Woman, remember? The secret is to know where you're going, and not to hesitate once you get there." I hugged her legs and rested my head on her hip, wondering how much starch it took to make her uniform so Monopoly-board stiff.

★ ★ ★

Baby Boomer approached us from behind the pine trees, an elegant young buck, silent and as illusory as a ghost. At a year and a half, he stood taller than Blossom and sported his first set of antlers. Bursting from nut-brown hairy nubs, they arched and divided into six soft and spongy velvety branches— that itched—really bad.

Those antlers were a real nuisance to him, and he spent a considerable amount of time dragging his forehead on the ground or trying to wipe them away with his feet. They also got caught on the dining room chairs, my legs, and under the front door handle, until he got the hang of the things.

It just so happened that my basement junk drawer held the remedy: a flexible freezer-ready gel mask with adjustable eye-hole sections that fit comfortably around a standard set of aggravating antlers.

The yearling bucks in the neighborhood had formed close-knit, reclusive bachelor friendships. Boomer was just like them, except he wore a rainbow collar and came home every day to visit his "other" family. Mostly Blossom. He was never far away from her. Never.

"*Neahhh* ..." Boomer greeted us.

"How're you, Boomer?" He lowered his head over Blossom and brushed his nose along her shoulder. This was their routine.

Much of her brittle hair had broken into prickly shafts, but also, here and there, patches of downy fur peeked out. Slowly, she lifted her head, looked at him through swollen eyes, and flicked her tongue across his nose.

One of the horses neighed from the back paddock, and a mourning dove awakened with something good to coo about. Blossom sniffed and ate a small amount of the food I prepared.

It was a start.

I hummed a song by Gene Autry, from a time, way before I ever dreamed I might be lucky enough to have a horse of my own or a deer who loved me.

Blossom always paid attention when I sang to her. I added a cowboy-like twang to the words.

"Have I told you lately that I love you?"

I cried quietly when the granola dropped out of Blossom's mouth.

Chapter 29

Extortion

My mind went blank after the first "Hello." Repugnance so instant and complete that I have no recollection of his words, my feelings, the time, or for how long I sat frozen at my desk.

Slowly, as if a mental dimmer switch eased me back into awareness, I strained to puzzle out what was happening.

He giggled a little, like before. "I have her— "She's right here."

Then, "Answer me!" The caller demanded. "Did you hear me?"

I pushed away from my desk, slowly stood. "Hu-hello … what?" I rolled my head from side to side to lessen the viselike grip on my windpipe.

I recognized his voice, knew the game he was playing, and yet, his words drilled into my heart. With each word, I pounded my fist on my desk.

"Leave us alone!"

"I'm not liking your tone so much. You understand that I can kill her as quickly as I can hang up this phone. You know I can. That would be sad, huh, Blossom?"

Is he talking to her?

"You should be humbled to do anything I ask you to do," he said.

Stunned by his arrogance, I said, "Humbled? What's your problem? That's it, isn't it? You're enjoying your playtime."

"You're going to give me twenty-five thousand dollars by Sunday, or she's d-e-a-d, dead." His words ended in a wheeze.

"You're crazy!" I wanted to throw the phone at the wall as if it were a grenade. *Where would I get that much money?*

"Don't get so excited," he continued in a matter-of-fact, unemotional attitude. "Poor Blossom won't experience a violent death. I'll bury the poison deep in the apple, much more of it this time. You don't want her to suffer long, do you?"

I shouted into the phone. "The poison is in your brain—"

"*Hmm*, not so much, I think." He muffled a cough. "You leave the money, unmarked, next to the Oldwick corn maze sign, or you'll never see her again. Your call."

By the corn maze sign? Ridiculous. He sounded arrogant—the idea, childlike and dangerous.

"You're lying. How do I know you have her?"

"Too late. Are you hearing me?" He laughed like a crazy person, spiraling out of control. "You want her ear as proof?" He faked a series of tiny squeals.

"No! Don't hurt her."

His wheezing became more pronounced, but he persisted. "It's her life, or—"

"Why do you do it? What made you so cruel?"

A short silence followed. With the phone jammed tight against my ear, I heard the muffled conversation that he was too late to block—a woman's voice, asking, "Invite her over."

A woman?

"Who are you?" I shouted a second before he hung up.

Impossible. Couldn't be. She sounded ... nice.

I auto-dialed Pino. It was noon. His meeting would go through lunch, then the seven-hour drive from Massachusetts. It would be dark by the time he got home. I left a message, "Call me. Pino! He called again. Says he has Blossom and wants twenty-five thousand dollars by Sunday, or he'll kill her."

I could not imagine how one person might grab a wild and unwilling Blossom, shove her into a vehicle, and confine her. Even sick and drugged, she would never give up without a fight.

He's a liar.

His urgency had changed the conversation this time. He could kill Blossom, no doubt. But, he was also hiding behind a phone and had gotten away with it far too long. A sadistic game player with a perverse thrill of probing, prodding, and stalking Blossom and our family.

Determined not to become a pawn in his game, I jotted notes of the conversation on a yellow legal pad and edited my thoughts to use in another police report.

Time and again, I thought about the unexpected woman who interrupted the phone call.

Who was she?

Chapter 30

Rose Cottage

I was out of time—out of choices.

I shuddered, not sure what scared me the most: that Blossom sought shelter within the damp shadows beneath old Rose Cottage, or the heartbreaking possibility that she was not there.

With syringes, food, and medications secure in my knapsack, I started up the time-worn path to her den. I focused my binoculars on the tumble-down part of the stone wall separating our farm from George's ivy-cloaked pink bungalow. Hidden behind a dense line of shrubs and trees, you would have to pay attention driving by Rose Cottage, or you'd miss it.

Odd, how the empty house appeared so tired and lonely. I missed our kindly neighbor, and the woodworking sounds coming from his workshop late into the night. George was at his son's home, recuperating from a second fall.

A few months ago, late in the afternoon, I followed Blossom to his overgrown garden while he trimmed long ivy tendrils from a front window. He allowed her to nibble. "She can have it all," he said.

George recalled, "Sixty-one years ago I built this house as a present for my bride. Only three houses on the street back then."

He chuckled. "Used to be called Pig Turd Alley. Bet you didn't know that juicy piece of local history, did you?"

It was wonderful to hear him laugh.

"We had so many friends and dandy times here," he sighed. "Pig Turd Alley? That wins for the worst name in the world to put on an envelope." I closed my eyes, imagining. Ultimately, I asked, "Why pink?"

A sudden sadness crossed his face, and he leaned over his cane to pet Blossom. She licked his hand.

I tried to take back my question and touched his arm, frail beneath the soft red and black plaid flannel shirt. "No, never mind, I'm sorry."

"Why …?" His voice cracked. "Because Emma loved pink. Simple as that. From day one, it was Rose Cottage to us. Fifty years ago, we added the wood deck around the little tree over there." He grinned and pointed to the massive poplar growing through the wood decking. "My wife viewed everything through rose-colored glasses." He smiled sadly.

"Emma would've been tickled by Blossom."

★ ★ ★

Surprised by the iridescent orange glint from behind the twelve-foot hedge, I zoomed in on Boomer, poking and twisting his antlers in and out of the bushes. A sure sign that he was itchy. He was growing fast and appeared at least fifty pounds heavier than Blossom, but at a year and a half, was never far away from her.

"Boomer!" I called and started across the diagonal of the hill. He lowered his head to be scratched. Other than remnants of velvety shreds hanging from his new antlers, he looked statuesque and healthy. Careful to avoid the bony points, I adjusted his rainbow collar and scratched his head.

She must be nearby.

Boomer followed me to the rear of the cottage, past arching branches of fragrant honeysuckle, to where planks of decking had buckled around the trunk of the poplar.

Between the deck and ground, across a wall of wood lattice, shadow art danced behind rows of sunset-colored dahlias. One section had broken off, leaving a dark, yawning entrance to the right of four worn steps, where Boomer waited.

Given a choice about where I would never go, crawling under an old house would top the list. I was tempted to stop, stretch, deep breathe, and procrastinate on just about anything else.

I secured my knapsack to the belt loop on my jeans to drag it, and crawled in.

Bright stripes of sunshine sliced through the overhead boards, creating a unique architectural birdcage-like grid over the poplar's bulky roots. Where planks had rotted and fallen away, slabs of sunlight allowed a surprising vertical oasis of minuscule mosses and wavy ridges of mushrooms to thrive around its root crown.

Blossom could stand here if she kept her head down.

The underbelly of old decking was downright spooky. Long nails protruded from supporting joists in places where someone had tried to stabilize the decking, and lopsided piles of old railroad ties obscured ambient light along the far wall.

Off to the right, a shallow, rectangular alcove was bricked into the original cement foundation, and fragments of clay pots lay in heaps, crumbled with age. I sat back on my heels and fought the urge to scuttle back into daylight.

"Boomer, you better be sure about this." I brushed a strand of cobweb from my face. He lowered his head, bent into the opening, and snorted. He might have followed me if his antlers hadn't hung up on the edge of the planking.

The dirt was cool with the subtle smell of a freshly dug garden. A movement out of the corner of my eye caught me off-guard, and I spun into one of the support beams.

"*Ow*!" I held my head and felt the swelling start at my temple. By squinting through one eye at a time, the pinpoints of pain eased.

"*Aehhh* ..."

"Blossom!"

Whatever was trying to kill her seemed to be winning. Shadows did not hide her bleary-eyed look or protruding ribs. Nor could they conceal her fluffy, wagging tail as she came closer. "Hello, sweet girl." She nested her nose in my palm. Her breath felt hot, feverish.

My fingers made swirls on her chest and traced down her slender forelegs to the pulses in her ankles. She allowed me to lift each foot and massage between her toes along the closely matched pressure points on the animal acupuncture chart I studied.

I convinced myself that the antibiotic, good nutrition, and care would cure her, given time.

Once in a while, time needed a helping hand.

Twenty minutes later, the horse chow and probiotic mixture she had been reluctant to eat were finished—so were the blueberries and the pint of milk.

"I knew you could do it."

She burped, went behind the tree trunk, and squatted.

"Hey, little Miss Modest," I said, marveling that her kidneys were still functioning well.

She came back and watched me fill and flick air from the syringes. "Just three little pinches, okay?" I probed for the thickest area of her rump muscle, slid the first needle in, and depressed the plunger. She flinched but didn't pull away from the next two injections.

"You'll be better now." I stroked her body. As usual, she comforted me, maneuvering for a better angle to lick the grime off my face.

If my heart could break, it would have happened then.

"Remember what I told you about staying away from creepy people?"

I kissed her goodbye. "I'll come back later."

The crunch of tires slowing on gravel startled me. It sounded close. Boomer took off. Blossom's ears didn't even twitch.

Filthy, bruised, and sore from crouching, I crawled out of the space, more optimistic about Blossom's recovery than I had been in weeks. It was past three o'clock. Pino should be out of his meeting.

Yay, three bars on the cell phone.

Half a ring later, the signal bars disappeared. My throbbing head upped its tempo from a waltz to a polka.

I'd have more luck with two soup cans and a string.

Next on my to-do list were a soothing hot shower, fragrant body wash, foamy shampoo, and the new cobalt bottle of miracle moisturizer that promised to do the impossible. *With all the ailments happening around here, a miracle could come in handy.*

I made my way across the section of rock wall where flat stones and old lilac bushes offered more substantial branches to steady myself.

Odd.

If its engine didn't sound like my dog scratching at the door to go out, I might not have noticed the car parked, half-hidden by the hedgerow. I waited. The engine shut down, but the driver did not get out.

Alarms went off when he finally started for my house. I recognized his agitated demeanor, the way he kicked the ground and jammed his fists in the pockets of the gray hoodie. It was the same person I saw from the hillside months ago. Only, this time, a heavy dog leash was draped around his neck.

My fingers closed around my cell phone and flipped it open. *Damn!* No signal.

Effortlessly, he jumped the three steps to my front door, rang the bell and knocked, the second time, louder. Satisfied that no one was at home, he moved to the alcove under the bay window—Blossom's place—and peered inside my bedroom.

He seemed familiar with our property, sauntering toward the backyard and tossing an apple from hand to hand. Methodically searching, he called out "Blossom," as if he knew her well. He skirted the paddock on the far side of the alpaca shed in an ever-tightening pattern.

The dread of recognition tingled at the nape of my neck. There was no doubt that soon he would see me crouching near the wall. I fought the urge to run away, hide.

Had she come to him before? Was that how he poisoned her—by being friendly, offering her an apple? Was the leash meant to drag her away?

My safety whistle was my weapon. That, plus adrenaline-driven anger, gave me the courage to run at him and divert his attention. I tripped, recovered, and continued toward him.

The long, siren-like whistle stopped him cold. "WHO ARE YOU?" I shouted.

He spun around, arms lifted in surprise, and backed away. A moment later, he was sprinting toward the street.

"HELP!" I screamed, hoping David might be working on his stone wall or that someone nearby was out riding or jogging.

"YOU! The police are on their way," I bluffed, pulling out my cell phone. I flipped it open, punched "000" with a flourish, and held the dead phone to my ear.

"HELP ME!" I screamed, then took a deep breath and blew the whistle three times. I rushed toward the house just in time to see his car lurch into gear, with David attempting to wave him to a stop with his trowel.

He jumped back as the car swerved around the corner and then ran toward me. "I heard the whistle. Are you alright?"

In a stream-of-consciousness blabber, I tried to explain. "He's going to kill Blossom if we don't give him twenty-five thousand dollars. He told me—he poisoned her before—with an apple."

"Oh, David," I continued, trembling. "He called to her, and ... he had an apple."

"It will be alright," he insisted, gently touching my face. "Call the police. Is Blossom safe? You're going to have a real shiner there. Get some ice on it."

"I banged my head—Blossom's under George's back deck. You know what we've been through. It will still be hearsay to the police," I said miserably.

A smile of satisfaction crossed his face. "Not anymore. I memorized the license plate number and saw the young man. I'm a witness. You can start there."

Chapter 31

Recon

The brass bells tied to my saddle were jingling loud enough to scare the bejeebers out of anyone near the hunting stand. That was the idea—no surprises—especially since it happened to be the first day of bow hunting season.

For perhaps the twentieth time in the last two days, I made up my mind to quit worrying and start thinking positively. But neither Blossom nor Boomer had come for breakfast, and I blew past my resolution, fast.

The megadose of broad-spectrum antibiotics worked its magic on Blossom. Within weeks, her body filled out, her undercoat grew in, and she regained strength with a ravenous appetite for yams, dandelion greens, corn, and granola. An equine veterinarian from the local teaching college suggested a tick-borne disease, possibly exacerbated by a weakened immune system from suspected poisoning, as the cause of her near-death experience.

Could he be the one who left the medicine?

"I am not her Fairy Godmother," the doctor assured me.

Typically, Blossom and a few older deer stayed closer to home during hunting season. Not Boomer. As his antlers grew and hormones surged, he spent long days socializing, traipsing through the woods, and engaging in mock battles with his buddies. Once, Pino bent down and found out the hard way what it felt like to be butted from behind.

"Don't squat in front of Boomer!" he said, brushing dirt off his jeans.

The controversy surrounding deer was growing. Some hunting enthusiasts were now Blossom's friends and protectors, while a few outspoken naturalists and gardeners were irritated by the presence of too many deer eating underbrush and picking through flower beds. Blossom had a fan club, no doubt. But Boomer? Trying to save two pet deer, was pushing the odds—and still no word on meaningful efforts to bring humane contraception to our area.

Time to recon the neighborhood.

The path next to the south side of the stream was now passable. Nearby, a fat raccoon peeked through her bandit mask and studied our slow meanderings.

"Hello, you," I said to the raccoon and watched idly as she continued to manipulate, dunk, and crack open a meal of nuts with her teeth and long, tapered fingers.

Justinian tugged the reins through my fingers, lowered his head for a long drink, and nuzzled through dried leaves, blanketing a patch of sweet winter clover at the water's edge. Last summer, I found a perfect four-leaf clover in this very place.

I remember Blossom sniffng as I twirled the little green shamrock under her nose. "Nope, not for lunch." I pointed to one leaf at a time. "One is for Faith ... the second for Hope ... the third for Love ... and the fourth makes magic ... it's for Luck."

We crossed the rock-strewn stream where it made a slow bend around three old pines. I dismounted and led Justinian over a downed branch until the hunting blind loomed ahead, twenty feet off the ground. It would have been a nice picnic area if I didn't know it was a death trap. The quiet tranquility of a gurgling stream—a sudden splash, perhaps the raccoon or a deer, behind me.

The foreboding structure had been spiffed up; someone had spray painted over rust spots on the feed baiter and replaced the camouflage awning. With some satisfaction, I noticed that the timed rotating gizmo continued to have lousy aim, and misfired portions of corn kernels at clusters of mushrooms at its base. Nevertheless, it meant doom for unsuspecting deer.

The only thing missing is a hanging plant.

Justinian anxiously pawed the ground.

"Scary, huh?" I absently fingered his reins and let my gaze drift to a sunny spot in the center of the clearing, where elongated patterns of red blood gleamed on kicked-away piles of decaying vegetation. The earth had been flattened, deeply gouged in places—and body imprints—where the animal fell, fought, and scrambled to escape.

God, let him be okay.

I looked up and stepped back as an awful sense of irony took hold. Under skies as serene as ancient stained glass in a house of worship, the plasticized poster of Blossom remained tacked to a broad oak as if for decoration. In bold print, the "Please Don't Shoot Blossom" message continued to plead for her life.

I mounted Justinian from one of the log benches. "Let's get out of here."

★ ★ ★

Later, it was back to work as usual, but with a growing sense of unease. I speared another bite of cantaloupe and focused on the intimidating twelve-page phone bill—the downside of maximizing our advertising dollars with a free 800 call-in number.

"Pino, I wonder. Do you think he called using the 800 number from our poster?"

"I considered that possibility, but how would we know?"

I stacked the pages and went to his desk. "Take a look. The new phone bill itemizes all incoming calls, categorized by state, time, duration, and date for the past month."

"When did they start that?" He took the invoices. "Do you remember what time he called?"

"Ten something ..." I brought the lined yellow legal pad from my desk and flipped through the pages. "Umm ... exactly 10:46 a.m."

"Here we go," he said, tracing the columns of data as if reading a thriller. Suddenly, he slapped the pages with the back of his hand. "It's a local number!"

"I'll drop this by the police station on my way into town," he said.

"You might also want to ask why they haven't called us. The police must have traced the license plate by now."

The phone rang—I let it ring. Pino took the call and gestured toward the window. He mouthed, "Blossom—something's wrong."

I nodded and went outside to see. The way she hesitated every few steps, kept her head low, stiff, and cocked to the side, was unnatural. Dried leaves and dirt clung to her usually sleek body. From ten feet away, I saw the nasty swelling on her face.

She flinched when I touched it. "Ouch! It's sharp." I tried to hold her back.

"What's sharp?" Pino opened the door.

"*Aehh* ..." She squeezed around him, cut through the office, and rumbled up the stairs to the kitchen—her safety zone.

"A splinter, I think. Forget tweezers, I'll need needle nose pliers and my medical kit," I said.

Forty-five minutes later, after setting up, the Banamine had calmed her. Pino sat cross-legged on the kitchen floor, and Blossom's head rested on a towel in his lap. Compresses of antiseptic washing solution followed by heated Lidocaine ointment flowed smoothly through gauze squares I held over the wound. Every few minutes, I dosed more liquid onto the patch of gauze with an eye dropper.

"Hey!" Pino readjusted his leg and shifted under Blossom's weight. "My jeans are soaked with that stuff—my leg is numbing up."

"Ready?" I poked at the lump in Blossom's jaw. She didn't pull away, only blinked with worried eyes.

Pino cupped one hand under Blossom's eye to block her view and held her foreleg loosely with his other, in case she kicked out. Magnifying glasses and a curved dental mirror allowed a view of the surprisingly smooth underside of the wood protruding from her jaw.

"If I angle it out, with pressure on the smooth side, it should come out easier." I locked the small spring-loaded pliers on the ragged end and, little by little, eased the splinter from her cheek, then dropped it on the floor.

"Is something that large still called a splinter?" Pino asked, picking it up.

I cleaned and smeared antibiotic ointment into the wound. "She'll be okay."

"Surprising." Pino examined the three-inch piece of wood closely and ran his thumbnail over the turquoise stripe. "Hand painted." He folded it carefully in a gauzy square, then a paper towel.

"Anyway, I have to get going. I'll bring a copy of that bill to the police."

That the caller lived close by horrified me.

Chapter 32

Hunter's Moon

It was late when I closed the doors to the barn and paused to watch a slice of cloud slide a frown over the face on the moon. A nocturnal owl hooted once, twice. Another owl answered softly. Behind me, the horses nickered and shuffled on fresh pine shavings, readying themselves for the night.

The October Hunter's Moon hung low in the sky, transforming Unicorn Hollow into a vibrant woodland of cobalt blue shadows that were edged in silver-dappled moonlight. I removed my gloves to touch the fresh, chilly air.

Four long weeks had passed since I saw the trail of splattered blood near the hunting blind.

Baby Boomer never came home.

Books dealing with grief and meditation helped, but I had a difficult time persuading myself to practice acceptance, patience, and forgiveness. But this night, the moon's dynamic energy seemed to brim over, tap into the consciousness of the earth. With my arms opened wide, I tried to connect from deep within myself to the movement of the earth, moon, and stars.

I had to ask.

Deep breath in, slow breath out. I closed my eyes and concentrated on the chilled air flowing into my lungs—the warmed air flowing out.

"Please ... his name is Boomer." I waited, peeked, squinting into the shadows for a subtle movement. Maybe tease out some hope that Boomer would step into the light—just because I asked.

Nothing.

I tried again, "Please, don't forget Boomer."

I reluctantly returned to the house, numbed with the fear that Boomer had been killed.

After dinner, Pino plopped on the sofa and lifted Kaya to his lap. Infused with the curative powers of the waltz music I grew up with, I swayed to our new surround sound system and danced to the same melody my mother had played on her piano. The same waltz I remembered humming while dancing around Viola's cubicle in the kids' ward. Smiling was a problem for her, so she mostly giggled. It was cute.

The Blue Danube Waltz ended. I bowed with a flourish and
    reached to tickle Kaya. She yipped, jumped off the sofa, and her fluffy tail went into overdrive. She scrambled to the front door. "Probably Blossom. Let's go see," I laughed at the pup.

Bright arcs of light shone from the front door lamps, making it impossible to see beyond, but the tippy-toeing clicks of deer feet over the bluestone meant we had company. Blossom came into the circle of light, absently licking at a new cut on her nose.

"How did you hurt yourself this time?" She raised her head for a kiss.

"Not a chance—until I clean you up."

"Did she reopen the same wound?" Pino handed me a paper towel. I spat on it and wiped her mouth.

"Don't do that. Remember germs?" Pino said. "Mine or hers?"

"Yours."

Blossom took a carrot from Pino, didn't bite down, but held it between her top palate and lower jaw, turned, and disappeared into the darkness.

Strange.

Early, before barn chores, I zipped up against the autumn breeze and took a brisk walk around the farm. Leaves of deep crimson and oranges were strewn everywhere, like the squares in a patchwork quilt. Blossom was under the maple when I returned to the front of the house, but this time—

"Boomer!" First, with relief, then bewilderment, I watched him struggle to his knees, hook his neck over Blossom's back for support, and stand. He dipped his head and snorted when I touched him. His antlers were all bone now, with six sharp points on each.

"Boomer, what happened to you?"

Keeping Blossom in the middle, I rested my hand on her neck and waited for Boomer to calm down. A minute later, he nuzzled my arm in an offer of peace. He never was much of a kisser. Up-down, up-down, he nodded against my curled, stiff fingers, held rake-like between his antlers.

Pino opened the front door, and a cup of hot coffee stopped midway to his mouth. "Boomer?"

"He injured his shoulder."

Often Boomer took a shortcut through the living room to the backyard. This time, he rested on each step before walking into the house, straightaway to the little pail of horse chow and apple slices we kept in the foyer. He walked with a terrible limp yet carried himself with the demeanor of a wounded soldier— composed and proud.

Blossom stayed outside, content to nibble on a grassy spot near the maple.

"He's so thin," Pino murmured. "Could he have been hit by a car?"

Boomer ate, drank some water, and then limped into the living room. Once, I half expected him to fall over, but he pivoted his left foot to its tip and remained standing on three legs.

The extent of his deformity became apparent only after I sat cross-legged, face to face, in front of him while studying the symmetry of his body. Swelling engulfed his shoulder completely, and his back appeared bulked up, twisted, and bent inward to the left.

"What's wrong with him?" Pino moved closer.

"Poor Boomer." I laid my hand on his chest. Before long, a wiggle of his nose tickled my forehead. "Let me loosen your collar." He rolled his foot forward.

"What the—"

I stared, trying to make sense of the dark object poking midway through the thick hair on his left shoulder. It didn't belong there. I touched it.

"Oh, God! Call Dr. Mike at the college. There's a nail, a big one, or maybe an ice pick sticking out of his shoulder!"

"Where?" Pino held the phone to his ear and knelt behind me to look. "No, not an ice pick," he whispered and laid his hand on my arm. "The tip of an arrow!"

The call went through. "Hi, Dr. Fugaro's office? Pino waited for the vet tech. "Tell him it's Pino. One of our animals was shot with an arrow.

"Yes. Deep in his shoulder. About an inch of metal is protruding.

"No, he's not a horse."

He did not say deer.

"Okay, thanks, I'll wait for the doctor's call."

"You think he'll come—for a deer?" Never far from my mind, the gut-wrenching triangle of fear linked hunting, the law, and the animals we loved. "I'll beg him, tell him this is different, a humanitarian emergency."

He grimaced. "He's at a farm on Homestead Road. I'll find him." Within a minute, his car pulled out of the driveway—too fast.

"You sleepy, Boomer?"

I didn't have a clue about weaponry. As far as I knew, arrows had triangular tips, wooden shafts, and feathers. This thing looked more like a spear. Where's the part with the feathers?

"Boomer," I nudged him. He glanced at me, yawned, and beelined it to his favorite spot near the baby grand.

"Come on, Boomer, no! Don't go there! Boomer, your antlers!"

My piano!

I held my breath and waited for the catastrophe to happen—except that it didn't. Boomer kneeled and inched his way under the piano to the vertical pedal supports, the way he used to do as a fawn.

Perhaps the puncture was shallow.

"Okay, Boomer. Let me see."

On hands and knees, I moved closer and spoke to him in chatty sing-song tones he was used to. "Remember the time you tried to climb the tree and the angry blue jay? You were a pushy baby; I told you that. Blossom loves you too; you know that, huh, Boomer? Don't worry; we'll fix you up."

My fingers rested in the soft space between his left elbow and chest wall, where I timed his breathing and heart rate. Not a drop of blood on him, no doubt thanks to Blossom.

But his eyes—full, glassy, and white-rimmed with fear—foretold the extent of his injuries. Never trust a large animal in pain. For safety, I moved behind the metal pedal bars next to his head.

"Boomer, Dr. Mike will help. Then you'll need antibiotics—with blueberries."

An ominous, guttural moan and deep trembling gripped his body. Suddenly, he stiffened; his eyes went blank and rolled up into his head.

"Boomer!" I pleaded as his body succumbed to an uncontrollable seizure—twitching, rolling, convulsing under my hands. The arrowhead ripped at my sleeve as I struggled to limit the side-to-side battering of his antlers.

He could die.

For an eternity-like moment, as if suspended in the eye of a storm, I stared at the hideous rod. With ruthless precision, the arrowhead protruded, pulsed, and thrust its triangular blade out of Boomer's defenseless body.

Not possible!

The arrowhead was not going into his shoulder—It was coming out of him!

At last, after what seemed like a ghoulish nightmare, the seizure ebbed. Confused, Boomer grunted and tried to roll to his belly. Eyes shut tight, tongue lolling out of his mouth in exhaustion, he shuddered through a deep breath.

"Boomer—okay—good boy. All over now." I pressed my arm against the widening blood stain on my shirt.

Where was the rest of it?

Getting shot through the body was not a survivable injury.

Of course! The same arrow cut Blossom's mouth when she groomed him. He survived after being shot because of her! She cleaned off the blood, tidied him up as she had been doing since he was a fawn.

I stretched over his spine, near his right hip, and felt for the dent that would confirm the entrance wound.

It has to be there.

My phone buzzed. I backed out, pulled the phone from my pocket, flipped it open. The husky voice of our vet crackled through.

"Mike? Did Pino reach you?"

"Going to be difficult. I can't come right away, but—" He didn't have to say more. He's not going to help! "What's going on?" he asked.

"Mike, do you remember Boomer, the little buck? He was shot straight through his back. I see the arrow. The whole thing is moving inside of him! He just had a seizure!"

Silence.

Did he hear me?

I wouldn't give him the chance to turn me down.

"Please. Wait. I have an idea! You don't have to touch him. All you have to do is take a look and tell me what to do—

"You can trust me. I can do it."

"Slow down," he said. "I'm on your side."

"Gosh, I'm so sorry for being a nudge, but—you're his only hope. He's going to die!"

"Can you coax him into the barn? He'll need a sedative. I've got to get a team together. Did you say that the arrow went through him?

"Unlikely. He'd be paralyzed. I'll need X-rays." He went through a checklist. "I'll bring the portable unit we use for horses."

I struggled to make sense of what he replied and inhaled sharply, "You'll come?"

"Yes, of course," he said. "Don't worry. I'm considering this a research project. Can you get close enough to inject a sedative into the deer?"

"Huh? Close enough? He's in the living room now, under the piano. His eyes are open and focused. He's breathing fine. Not much pain when he stays still. The seizure exhausted him."

"The buck is ... under the piano?" Mike asked with a touch of wit.

I had gushed out every emotion from A to Z without giving him a chance to get a word in edgewise. "Thank you. Thank you so much for caring."

"Glad to help. I'll be there shortly."

My hand on Boomer's leg shook slightly.

"Boomer, you'll be okay. It won't be long now. The doctor is coming."

His great dark eyes begged for reassurance. "Dr. Mike will take that thing out of you."

Chapter 33

Arrowhead

Waiting for Dr. Mike to arrive was agony. I tapped on the window, leaned my forehead against the refreshingly cold glass, and thought of happier days when Blossom and Boomer were fawns not worth killing.

Clumps of amber-hued leaves dangled from the inner branches of the maple. Amongst the deer grazing across Wildwood, Blossom's collar left no doubt as to who she was.

She snapped to attention as if waiting for the invite, stopped to look both ways before crossing, and trotted toward the house. I held the door open.

It was no coincidence that Boomer was shot on the first day of hunting season. He was a trophy target; he had antlers and a collar, and he was friendly and well-known. Perhaps he dilly-dallied while the bow curved, string tightened, eye and arrow aimed to kill.

Behind me, Boomer's feet *click-click-draag-click'd* across the wood floor with the abnormal gait of a wounded animal. They bumped noses. He leaned against her as she cleaned his puffy eyes, deliberately taking special care around the base of the arrowhead.

I stared at her gentle kindness with a feeling so powerful I ached. A reminder that small gestures can often have the most impact. I went to the kitchen for a bag of baby carrots. A door slammed, followed by a series of thumps and clacks, as latches to the mobile clinic's supply compartments were opened and closed.

I called downstairs to Pino, "Mike's here."

"How are you?" Dr. Fugaro walked swiftly around the side of his truck, an orange needle cap held between his teeth. "You're sure about the arrow?" He flicked air bubbles out of the syringe before recapping and handing it to me. "This is a strong sedative. You have the honors. He doesn't know me."

"Has to be an arrow. When he moves, the metal tip protrudes from his shoulder." I gave him a bag of baby carrots. "Give him a few of these. Ah … and, don't bend down too fast."

He glanced at me, surprised. "Where is he?"

"In the house, with Blossom."

The reality of Boomer as his patient was sinking in. "Hard to believe."

They studied each other from a distance.

Boomer didn't attempt to rise but remained on guard when Mike eased his way toward him, knelt, and studied the wound.

"So, you're Boomer." He opened his hand. "Here, I have something for you." Intuition, carrots, and the doctor's soothing bedside manner did the trick. Boomer relaxed and allowed Mike to scratch his chin.

"Should I get wine bottle corks for his antlers?"

"I don't think that's necessary, but we are going to need help. Two of my student techs have volunteered. Told them to swing by the office for the portable X-ray unit."

I took his hand. "Thank you."

He blushed, uneasy with the compliment.

"Are you okay with helping him? You won't get in trouble?"

"Stop right there," he waved, dismissing the idea with a wave. "There was no way I wouldn't help an animal in his condition. Besides, I'm treating this as a research project, remember?"

Pino brought a heavy, worn blanket from the basement. "I knew this thing would come in handy one day."

"Might be time to get Blossom outside while you give the sedative to the buck. Let him relax a few minutes while I unload supplies and make a few phone calls." He touched Blossom's ear. "Let's go." She followed him.

"Go figure," Mike called out. "My dog doesn't listen as well as she does."

Boomer grunted, struggled to his feet, and tried to follow her. I slipped the needle into his rump. He fought the effects of the sedative, shaking his head hard enough to make his ears flap, and wobbled forward, leaning heavily on his weak shoulder.

"I can't hold him." I strained to pivot his weight toward his right side, away from the wound.

"Okay, okay ... slowly." Pino crisscrossed his arms under Boomer's hind end and guided him to the blanket in a controlled collapse. "He must weigh two hundred pounds."

Boomer groaned.

"Lay him down!" I said. "The arrow is sucking back into his chest."

Boomer lay stretched on his right side, gasping for breath, his heart pounding so hard I could hear it. The sedative was finally forcing his body into submission. He sighed and closed his eyes, and his breath came in longer, easier puffs.

There was a soft knock before Mike walked into the foyer, followed by two veterinary students, both loaded down with medical supplies. "Melanie and Jo volunteered. We need some muscle," he said by way of introduction.

Melanie was cute, impish. She had hazel eyes, freckles, a dimpled smile, and curly red hair pulled tight off her face.

"Thanks for helping." I couldn't resist asking. "Are you Irish?" "Polish," she giggled.

"Close enough. Come in. We're all set up in the living room."

"Deer in the house?" Jo rolled her eyes toward the sky. "Note to self. I must be dreaming." She placed the portable X-ray machine near Boomer's rear, then set about unwrapping a tray of surgical instruments.

Flipping a stethoscope around his neck, Mike began a preoperative check: pulses, breathing, body sounds, and palpating his furry, white belly. "Heart and lungs sound strong," he said.

Melanie lugged cumbersome radiation aprons into the house, one for each of us. From his position at Boomer's belly, Mike glanced left to right, a quarterback checking his team.

"On three, roll him toward me so I can slip an X-ray plate under his chest. Pino, get a firm grip on those antlers."

Shh ... click, shh ... click ... One click per image from a handheld remote.

"Let's see what we're dealing with here. Melanie, I need another set of forceps from the truck." She went to the door and then poked her head back in.

"There's another deer at your front door. This is great!" Melanie lifted her shoulders in excitement.

"Meet Blossom," Mike said, with I-told-you-so written over his face.

Mike cleared his throat and studied the thumbnails of radiographs on the display unit. He touched one of the squares to expand the image to full screen.

"Let me show you something." His finger traced the outline of the straight, pencil-thick rod. "This is wood. Metal looks bright white on an X-ray. Interesting ... the back end of the arrow is gone." Mike expanded the image. "The wood appears shredded."

The next X-ray glared like a scene from a nightmarish sci-fi movie. There were murmurs of dismay.

"What are those things?" I pointed to two white elongated triangles lying within inches of each other.

"The blades of the arrowhead broken from the main rod, possibly deflected off a rib. The third blade is still attached to the rod," Dr. Mike said.

"And they keep moving as he breathes?" I asked. Gentle Boomer did nothing to deserve this.

The doctor's hand hovered above Boomer's back and hip in an almost reverent motion.

"The arrow entered here, missed his spinal cord by no more than a millimeter, skimmed the top of his lung before cutting across his back and partially exiting through the shoulder. Could be about fourteen inches still in him.

"Given the angle and the trajectory through his back, he was shot from above." Mike drew an imaginary line, crosswise with the side of his hand, through Boomer's back.

Bowed in thought, he said, "He's been skewered. Do you understand that the potential consequences of removing this arrow could be fatal? An organ, artery, or vein could be pierced." We glanced at one another, then back at him.

"We know." I grimaced.

There was a brief silence. Mike leaned closer to the screen. "There may be a fragment of wood embedded in the top of one lung. That will have to stay. The chest wall seems intact, but ..." Mike shook his head and slumped forward over his knees.

"Impossible. He's still struggling with the sedative. Never seen an animal survive anything like this."

"Never?" My heart sank.

Mike sighed and slapped his hand on his knees. "I hate being wrong, but I can't operate. He should be deep asleep by now. This drug might not have been the best choice, for a deer."

"But ... you said he couldn't live with an arrow in his back either, Mike," I pleaded. "Those blades can cut into his vital organs ... one twist could—"

"We understand he could die," Pino added softly.

"This is so not right." Mike slid his fingers under Boomer's collar, discouraged. "What kind of person would shoot an animal wearing a collar?"

Boomer stretched—the arrow rose. He moaned.

As if trying to convince himself, Mike spoke under his breath. "For a month, his body has been trying to encapsulate and expel over a foot of arrow that would have killed ninety-nine percent of anything alive. That he survived is incredible. I'll bet he has more than luck going for him."

Silence. Nobody looked at anybody else.

"Listen, he's tough, and besides ..." A wry smile started at the corners of his mouth.

"Okay." He pulled a tiny bottle from his bag, poked a needle through the rubber top, and drew back on the plunger. "This is the last of the sedative. He's had twice the horse dose. This one is going straight into his jugular vein."

This time, Boomer didn't resist the gentle, steady pressure of Pino's hand on his head or the deep poke of the needle.

"Give him a minute," Mike said and stood to stretch.

The rubbery snaps of Latex surgical gloves broke the silence. "All set?" Mike looked at each of us, then at the ceiling. "Pass me the shaver, please, Jo."

The blades buzzed and shaved through Boomer's undercoat, leaving a three-inch square patch of skin around the arrowhead, dead center. He cleaned the skin with antiseptic and dried it.

"Anna, hold his front legs down. Keep the pressure on his hip. Melanie, what do you make of this?" he questioned his students.

"It may be a type of broadhead hunting arrow," Melanie said. "You can't pull back without damaging everything behind it. Will you have to open his back?"

"Nope. I'm going to help finish what his body started."

Under my hands, Boomer's legs twitched as if he were moving in a dream. Pino held his head by his antlers, cradling his face in his arms.

"Scalpel." Mike held out his hand.

"Scalpel," Jo repeated. The precision slap of the surgical instrument was, in some respects, comforting.

Someone else was in control.

"Let's extend the exit wound ... like sooo." The skin split behind the scalpel. "From here, across the top of the arrow, to the right ... about ... here. Then another cut to form a V... to give me more space to find those loose blades."

Jo dabbed at the incisions with a thick square of gauze.

"Easy ... steady ... feel for the angle of least resistance," Mike spoke more to himself as he deftly locked a clamp on the rod. "The challenge is going to be to keep this simple. Get it out without doing more damage."

The arrow didn't move. It was stuck.

"Ah, geez." As if weary, Mike closed his eyes, shook his head and sighed.

My gaze drifted from Boomer to Mike's white-gloved hands as he nimbly maneuvered surgical pliers, twisting in small increments as if winding an old wristwatch. "Ready," Mike said. "Here we go again. Hold him."

It was dead quiet as the doctor carefully coaxed and guided the arrow from Boomer's pinkish flesh, following the same trajectory it had taken when it pierced his back. The silence persisted until a series of sucking and popping sounds signaled the arrow's release from sinew and scar tissue.

Inch after inch of natural-grained wood emerged. It appeared coated and waxy. Close to the nine-inch mark, the color changed to a vibrant turquoise. Except for the empty scar where the wood had peeled to its natural core, the turquoise encircled the shaft like a stripe.

At last, smoothly, the arrow was pulled free from Boomer's body. It was held up, harmless, held fast in the forceps. Mike stared at it. "What do you think? Fourteen inches?"

He probed deep into the wound for remnants of wood and metal. First with forceps, then with gloved fingers. "Found one." He maneuvered a slick razor-sharp blade into the light and placed it on a gauze square. Another minute passed, and the second of the triangular blades was removed.

"The arrow came out clean—no excessive bleeding, no problems. I'm ready to stitch him up." He checked Boomer's heart, lungs, and the pulses in his legs.

"Good job, people." He nodded. "Let's watch him for a while in here, and then we'll try to carry him outside. He's a big guy."

"He'll be better waking up in the house," I suggested. "Rain is forecast—"

"Or, he could take out your dining room when he tries to stand," Mike said.

"I agree with Mike." Pino was adamant. "Let's also consider making him less of a trophy by cutting off the ends of his antlers." Dr. Mike didn't seem to like the idea. "We might have to wait."

"Can I keep the arrowhead?" I asked.

He studied each section and then handed the three metal pieces to me. "See how the blades fit into these narrow slots? This thing is quite a weapon, made to destroy. It comes in spinning."

Mike saw the expression on my face. "Listen, what you have to keep telling yourself is that he's alive. It's all good."

★ ★ ★

I sat next to Boomer on a small corner of the blanket. It had taken him almost half an hour to wake, but he couldn't keep his tongue in his mouth. I massaged his ears and the soft area over his temples. The arrow shaft lay atop the square cloth amongst surgical waste. Benign now. A simple weapon. I picked it up and rolled it between my fingers. It didn't wobble.

Hateful thing.

The edge of the stripe appeared thicker, as if hand-painted— turquoise, a good color for a piece of jewelry. Perhaps the hunter was a woman, maybe even a mother, who constructed the arrow herself and chose its color scheme to match its feathers.

I rolled the arrow between my thumb and forefinger, faster and faster, until the torn-away piece seemed to fill the gap with missing color.

Pino took the arrow. "This color," he mused. "Wait ..." He went to the kitchen and returned with a folded square of paper toweling. "I'll let you know in a second."

"You saved the splinter?" I asked.

Pino held it up. "We removed this from Blossom's cheek." Even before he passed it around for comparison, we all knew.

It was as obvious a match as the last puzzle piece fitting seamlessly into the only remaining space in a picture.

The last question still hung in the air.

"Is it possible? Let me see," Mike said, bringing a small magnifying glass from his pocket. We stared, enthralled, as he examined the arrow and then joined the pieces.

"This explains the cuts on Blossom's mouth," Pino said.

"*Whew!*" Mike shook his head, murmuring, "Your evidence. I'll bet she was with him when he was shot. They got away. She chewed the shaft until it snapped and splintered into her cheek.

"There can be no other explanation."

Jo stared at him, surprised. "She tried to save him? A deer saving a deer? Never heard of it."

Mike seemed lost in thought. "Astonishing ... think about it. Her species survive because they can run away, yet she stayed with him."

It was dusk when a car pulled into our driveway.

"Oh, no, the police," Melanie said with a sense of urgency. "No!" I spun back to Mike in alarm. "The police," I whispered.

The police! We were going to be caught with a wild animal in the house and, worse, a vet who might now have a problem with the law.

All my fault!

Dr. Mike was bending over Boomer, glanced up, and shrugged. "So?"

"Quick, I'll cover Boomer." I grabbed a wool throw from the back of a chair and scrambled to put it over his antlers. "We can say he's an alpaca!"

"Ah-huh, right." Mike grinned and pushed the cover aside.

Pino was at the front door. I heard laughter.

Things were never terrible when Blossom was involved. True to form, our social butterfly was licking the officer's hand while he tried to maintain his most professional demeanor. He stepped into the foyer with the bearing of a man who had been in the military.

Blossom rubbed her nose across his knee.

"I've known Blossom a few years." The officer looked past Pino and saw Mike. "Hi, Doc. You're busy, so I didn't want to disturb you. Saw your truck."

"Perfect timing, Sarge," Mike said. "I could use another hand lifting the buck out to the garden."

"The buck? Sure thing, Doc."

Sarge turned his attention to Pino. "I want to talk to you about the status of another matter. I'll come by tomorrow."

"Sarge, come take a look at my patient." Mike cleared his throat and showed him the arrow.

The police officer gently stroked Boomer's ear, a wan smile on his face. He remained quiet for a while. "I'm trying to make sense of the senselessness of it. Why would anyone shoot an animal wearing a collar?"

Pino gazed at him, shaking his head sadly. "Somebody who can't imagine a deer with a name, a heart, and a life."

"On three, lift him." Mike quarterbacked the move to the garden.

It was close to midnight when Dr. Mike, Pino, and Sarge moved a very sleepy Boomer to the protected section of the garden near our office.

"He's a survivor." The doctor smiled.

The air was chilly, so I covered him. He kicked his blanket off twice.

A good sign.

Chapter 34

Sarge

The vibrating wrist alarm jolted me from sleep to wide awake shortly before dawn. It was my turn to check on Boomer. I pulled fleece pants over my pajamas, slipped into shearling boots, and tiptoed down the dimly lit hallway. A bag of medical supplies and my jacket were on a chair in the living room.

A minute later, I was at the patio door—ready, quick, and according to plan. I flicked on my light and stepped outside into a cloud-like fog. The diffused blast of light created close to a total whiteout, rendering the flashlight and me useless.

I can do this blindfolded. Navigate the patio and the furniture.

"Boomer," I called in a low voice muffled by the mist. I judged the distance to the stone staircase—eight small steps.

Zombie-like, I shuffled, arms outstretched, hands groping for one of the supporting poles of the pergola. Crash. A wrought iron chair grated across the bluestone. Maybe five small steps?

Ow!

Toe first, inching carefully forward, I collided with the three-frog "Welcome to My Pad" garden sculpture. It clunked on a boulder and landed with a thud seven feet below.

So much for my navigating skills.

Weather lore says for every dense fog in October, there will be a massive snow event in winter. We're going to get walloped with a real doozy.

"Boomer," I called a little louder, held tight to the bag over my shoulder, and slid my boot over the edge of the first step, then the next. The fog smelled wet, stale, and snugged closer the farther I descended. Now and again, I could see the moon. A horse neighed, another nickered, and small hairs prickled across my neck. No one could frighten me as much as I could.

Remnants of Boomer's bandages were strewn about, discarded, and muddied. His blanket hung limply across one of the boxwoods. A shadowy movement on the rise near the pool fence caught my attention. I heard shuffling, and then dry leaves crackling—close—next to me.

"*Neahhh* ..." Distorted by fog, his call sounded hollow but close.

"Boomer?" I gasped, dropped my bag, and knelt next to him. "You're as sneaky as a ghost."

Once my eyes adjusted, I checked the shaved entrance and exit wounds on his back. There was no significant swelling. He winced when I touched the prickly ends of the stitches.

Slightly off-balance, he stumbled to his feet and headed for the house. By the time I inched my way back up the stairway, he was waiting at the patio door. Blossom was there too, licking the ointment from Boomer's back—caring for his wounds the natural way. I slid open the door and let them both into the living room.

"Blossom, don't touch." I started the cleaning and bandaging process over again.

Blossom wanted to go back out while Boomer curled down, nose tucked between his hind legs, and fell asleep under the piano.

★ ★ ★

It took a little over a week for Boomer to return to his rambunctious self. He was thinner, ate well, slept more, and his wounds healed fast. We took advantage of a spell of crisp, sunny days to play, relax, and share the sweet corn Pino bought from a local farm.

"These won't last long." Pino yanked the husk and silks from an ear of corn, flipped, and snapped them off at the base. The tug-of-war shenanigans between Boomer and Blossom were hilarious, dodging, rearing, and trying to outmaneuver each other for the prize. With one yank, Boomer tossed the corn over his back, prancing like a high-stepping pony, teasing Blossom into another go'round.

"Mmm..." I made a big deal of the corn-on-the-cob experience, pulling the silky tassel-zippers and tugging the husks off.

My taste buds popped with the first sweet bite of the plump, succulent kernels.

"I started it for you." I gripped both ends of the corn, rotating as Blossom chomped, left to right, with the clunky motion of an old typewriter carriage. She chewed from side to side, her molars working in a figure-of-eight motion.

"Like she's playing the harmonica," Pino laughed.

Later, Pino had just finished replacing another poster on the oak near the barn gates when a police car pulled up, the window opened, and Sarge's ruddy, friendly face appeared.

"Hey, our favorite officer," Pino greeted him. "Have a few minutes to talk?"

"Sure, come on." Pino pulled both gates open and motioned Sarge to drive in. He waved the remaining poster. "I've replaced these a dozen times. We hope they're becoming collector's items."

"Can I have one for the station?" He appeared rested, scrubbed, police-crisp. "How's the patient?"

"Wonderful." I grasped his hand in both of mine. "Thanks for your help. It would have been tough moving Boomer without your muscle. I have to confess something, Sarge. I was unsure about trusting the police ..."

He cleared his throat and focused on his polished boots. "I know. Hey, I'm sorry, too. It took too long to understand what you people were going through."

I smiled. Pino frowned.

"So, we owe you some answers," Sarge appeared uneasy, a tinge of worry pulling at the corners of his mouth.

"You found the stalker?" Pino asked.

"Yes. But ..." He took a deep breath and frowned. "It's complicated. He's a frightened, troubled kid. Lives with his grandmother. Realizes he's in deep trouble and is panic-stricken that he could be prosecuted. It would break the old lady's heart."

"Frightened? I don't remember him behaving like a scared, concerned kid, do you?" I sounded bitter but resigned.

Pino glanced at me, obviously at odds with Sarge's assessment.

"How old is this person?" I asked.

Sarge took a notepad from his back pocket. "Late teens. No prior record. We're going to keep tabs on him, get him help. He knows that if he gets out of line, he's had it. His family is shaken and trying like hell to pull together to help him through this. I suggest you leave the matter in our hands."

"How? By giving up?" I shifted on my feet. He's asking me to trust him—I'll be awake at night forever.

"No, no," I said. "Too late to talk about his caring, Sarge. He knew what he was doing. How do we forget the fear of being stalked, his death threats to Blossom, and the demand for ransom? For God's sake, he admitted to poisoning her. Tell me how to make those fears go away? Poof!" I snapped my fingers. "Like that? Gone!"

"I know, I know." Sarge raised his arms in frustration. "It disturbs me, too. All I'm suggesting is that you give this kid a chance. He's got personal issues, his own demons to deal with."

"Come on, Sarge," Pino persisted. "I understand the rationale to help someone with a problem—we're all for that, especially if you're involved. Can you guarantee he won't do it again?"

I hesitated but needed to know. "Does this troubled kid have a gun?"

Sarge did not meet my eyes. "Not now."

I glared at him. "Not now? Don't you see something wrong with that?"

"It was his father's rifle. Let's be fair—"

"Wait!" I turned away, struggling with the realization. The idea of a gun in the hands of anyone unstable—or just having a bad day—terrified me.

"There's a huge disconnect between the words fair and guns. Are you saying that he had a gun while all this was going on, and we should assume that everything is going to be hunky-dory?"

Sarge reached into his shirt pocket and withdrew a folded piece of notepaper. He handed it to me. In a neat, round scrawl, the teen had written:

I will not hurt Blossom, and I don't want money.

I am sorry for all the hurt I have caused.

Freddie S.

I groaned and rolled my eyes. "How sweet."

"His grandmother wants to meet you." I detected a faint, hopeful tone in his voice.

My back stiffened. "You're kidding." I offered a wry smile. I remembered the woman's voice in the background, saying, "Invite her over." She sounded nice. "Oh, sure thing. Let's invite them over for tea."

"Not now, I don't think so," Pino said.

"I'm sorry," I apologized for my sarcastic remark. "Sarge … it's just that I'm … scared."

"Scared?" Sarge raised an eyebrow at me. "I understand. But, the problem is not only this kid. You know that." He stepped closer. "The truth is that I'm telling you this because I've seen your relationship with these deer. Most people around here consider Blossom a good luck charm. But, a few guys out there are making it known that they don't like the idea of being told not to pull the trigger."

"Oh, come on. Those guys know I'm asking for consideration for the pet deer, the ones with the collars. The same animals that will pose for a picture with their families, for a kind voice and a carrot."

"Look, I'm not defending them, but you might as well face it," Sarge said. "There's an angry conversation going around about who has the rights to Boomer. You, or the person who shot, tracked, and lost him. I must say, there is some sympathy for the second line of reasoning."

"For heaven's sake! They're a part of nature—not property. Ridiculous!" I blurted, sick of hearing the truth.

"There will always be a few loose cannons aimed at bragging rights on a trophy deer. Those collars you made may protect them from some folks. To others—you gave them the targets."

He's right.

"True," Pino said, breaking the awkward silence. "Maybe this is the best we can hope for, given the circumstances."

"I'm sorry, Sarge. I know that some hunters, not all, feel like that. I'm still amazed. We asked them not to shoot Blossom—and they didn't. Many became her friends."

"More than that," Pino added, "those same hunters protected her." He grinned, attempting to lighten the conversation. "I trust you. So, okay. Let's agree to take a chance on helping," he lowered his voice, "the kid."

"Don't forget, we have your number on speed dial," I added. Sarge shook his hand, relieved.

★ ★ ★

Deep into the night, somewhere in the distance, not too far away, I listened to the mournful wails of a dog. A sad rolling moaning that continued, according to the digital clock on my night table, for ten minutes.

I remembered another dog howling like that.

I was a child, barely able to see over the kitchen table in my grandmother's apartment in Brooklyn. My chunky fingers gripped the edge of the plaid vinyl tablecloth at eye level. Grandma's face had wrinkles so deep they cast their own shadows.

She was happy and busy cleaning mushrooms she had gathered on a day trip to the Berkshires, the mountains that reminded her of Vilnius and her home in Lithuania. Her kitchen always smelled musky, reminding me of wet wool.

My grandma called me Anja.

"Anja, Anja." Her soft voice promised peace and calm, yet her eyes betrayed sadness. She placed her small knife on a wooden board and gazed up at the frilly glass ceiling light, following the dangling tassel on the pull chain all the way to its tip.

I sensed her mood by the way her fingers drummed on the table, one at a time, and how she rocked in her stiff-backed chair. She folded her hands over the bib of her apron, the one with the hand-embroidered rose over the heart.

"What's the matter, Grandma?" I moved closer to lay my head against her arm.

She paused. "Oiy, oiy, oiy, Anja. A dog howl very loud last night. He cries ... like this." She lifted her head toward the ceiling and shoved her chin out to show me how the dog sounded. She was so good at the howl—it sounded so sad—I shivered.

"Someone is going to die." She knew this from what she called "the old country." Her premonition was right. My uncle Billy, a firefighter, died the next week. He was forty-two.

The dog howled again, jarring me from my memory.

Sleep was impossible. I slipped into a fleece turtleneck, jeans, my warm hooded coat, boots, and gloves. Blossom was on the back patio where she watched us walk from room to room. I opened the door, stepped out, and gazed at the luminous river of stars in our Milky Way Galaxy.

"*Aehh* ..."

"Did you hear the dog crying too, Blossom?"

She gazed at me with a depth of feeling that sent a tingle down my spine—as though she understood.

Chapter 35

A Place In The Choir

For days, we wove ropes of pine and holly into garlands, twisted and stuffed rolls of tiny lights through floppy red bows, and so edged the roof, the doors, and almost every window, gate, and walkway of our home.

My fingers were sore, but the decorations were dazzling—time to take a holiday picture "suitable for framing," as Mary would say.

The headband I crafted for Blossom's sixth Christmas was a stunner, adorned with elegant burgundy velvet and gold lamé ribbons, silky gardenias, cherry blossoms, and plenty of berries. She could have easily shaken it off, but she seemed to relish our playful game with the hat—first on my head, then on hers, before trotting off to the mirror, where I imagined she admired herself.

"Whatever happened to last year's snowflake crown?" Pino teased. "The one resembling the Statue of Liberty struck by lightning? Or the light-bulb headband? What about the furry, sequined rat-faced creation she hated?" His face brightened to match his jacket.

"You shouldn't joke around when you're on a ladder," I said. "Besides, it was a beaver, not a rat. Come to think of it, I may still have a picture worth throwing out someplace. You didn't like the monster-mouse look, huh?"

"I'm never taking these down," a grumbling Pino countered, hoisting and wiring the final section of garland to the house. He lowered his bag of tools and descended the ladder. "No kidding," he insisted. "We ditch the bows and add flowers in the spring—grow a vine over the rest."

"Oh, I don't know. My thinking is that too much is never quite enough when it comes to Christmas decorations."

I made a thermos of hot buttered rum, dressed Kaya in a red plaid doggie coat, and tied a bow to her collar. Still behaving like a pup at close to seven years old, she yipped for attention, her curlicue tail fluttering nonstop, betraying any pretend patience for me to lift her.

"Her feet are cold." I unzipped my parka and stuffed her small body next to my chest for warmth.

"Are you ready?" Pino asked.

"Almost. Where's Blossom?" I poured him a mug of hot buttered rum and handed over the remote control.

"She was here earlier," Pino said.

I glanced around but didn't see her.

"Ready? Three, two, one—" And then, the jaw-dropping moment happened, when a gazillion twinkling lights, probably visible in space, turned on.

Momentarily stunned, Pino laughed. "Yahoo!" He stepped back to admire the spectacle. "You wait a long time to see something like this."

"Sweetness, we gift-wrapped the house!" I poked him in the arm and wiped tears of laughter from my cheeks.

"Lucky that's done. More snow tonight—the big one's coming." He warned.

The Weather Channel proved right. Snow flurries started at seven and intensified throughout the night. Twenty inches, windswept into eight-foot drifts against the barn, rounded every angle, blunted every point with easy-to-shovel, feather-like flakes.

We always cleared a path for the alpacas to play—from their shed, past the horse barn, winding between the poplars toward the house. They chased each other on the loop-de-loop track. Tinkerbelle, Huckleberry Rose, China, and America usually followed close, squealing and pronking with arched backs and stiff legs, all four feet off the ground, heads pointed downwards. Tinkerbelle often jumped off the path into deep snow, waddling like a colossal marshmallow come to life when we pulled her out. Morning dawned crisp and brilliant. It was an I-wished-my-pajamas-had-feet kind of day. Unicorn Hollow, usually a medley of rustlings, pawings, and murmurings, seemed unusually quiet. And yet, if you paid attention, everywhere, little eyes blinked from sheltered spaces, and quick shudders rid snow-covered fur and feathers into mini-poofs of white.

A family of squirrels played tag along pine-coned branches, and a pair of industrious red-crested Pileated woodpeckers whacked at a tree nearby—the larger of them hammering at a hole with a view at the top. He flapped and called a loud, rolling *kuk-kuk-kuk-kuk* at a couple of younger birds perched on an adjacent branch.

I scanned the hillside through the window's reflections. Bubble lights and mismatched glass ornaments spiraled to the top of the Christmas tree behind me. Within the tree's strongest branches, a string of eight toy soldier drummers struck up the band, playing tunes of the season. Each drummer spun with mighty gusto, striking at side-by-side tuned brass bells and finishing with Auld Lang Syne, before starting over in a never-ending loop.

Should auld acquaintance be forgot, and never brought to mind?

Never was a melancholy tune so upbeat.

Blossom was near her den, looking my way, watching from her "wild" side of the street. I waved. Claire and Sweet Pea stood nearby. Buckaroo too. No doubt, Boomer was off gal-livanting with his friends. I thought about his playful nature: tough, fun, and, with a little luck, a dream come true for the young does.

Blossom saw me. Head raised, nose up, sniffing, her tail flaring, she zigzagged down the trail.

She reached the mailbox just as I opened the front door.

Pino was enjoying a cup of coffee, toast with pomegranate jam, and his favorite newspaper. "What's up?" He approached.

"Blossom's here. Be right back. I'm going out."

"Take this." He passed me the toast. "I'll make more."

After folding my pajama cuffs above my ankles, I stepped into tall, shearling boots, grabbed my jacket and hat and went to join her. I sensed it odd but didn't give much thought to the reason Blossom waited by the mailbox just then.

Our overzealous mail carrier must have prepared for the storm. The metal door hinge was jammed shut. It squeaked when I pulled it open, and snow whisked across the lid and a stack of Christmas cards.

"*Aehh* ..." Rising on her hind legs, Blossom pulled at the mail. Two tugs and much of it scattered. A deep grunt, her body tensed, and she was at it again, probing into the box. Her left foreleg hit the pole and slipped off, but she kept on.

Her forcefulness took me by surprise.

"You're going to hurt yourself." I pushed her away, but she shoved by me, ignoring my concern.

I didn't understand—this was not a game anymore.

Suddenly, she stiffened and pulled out what she was after, shaking it violently, snorting, and tossing it over her head.

Boomer's collar landed in the snow.

Every fiber of Blossom's body quivered. The hair on her neck and back stood straight up, eyes and ears scoping the woods in panic.

"NO—NOOO!" Stunned, I froze.

"*AEHH ... AEHH ...*" her throat clogged with grief. The high- pitched terror of Blossom's scream echoed from the hills. The other deer jerked to attention, birds quit chirping, and squirrels were on alert.

I picked up the collar, shook the snow from it, and touched the bloody stain smeared over the band of colors meant to pro- tect him. My heart ached.

Who was the person who reeked with such contempt that he trum- peted his killing this way? Making sure we would know he had the power to harm an innocent animal?

"BOOMER!" I sobbed to the sky. "BOOMER!"

The snow began again, this time as if Mother Nature blew a goodbye kiss and fluffed a blanket over the buck who had learned to accept and tolerate humans and would be no more.

Blossom's expressive brown eyes were fixed on mine, intense, knowing. She blinked once, twice, shook tiny pyramids of snow from her ears, and finally let the snow stay.

"Boomer," I whimpered and traced a line down the center of her forehead, circling the white hairs around her nose. Then, I lingered on the velvety area behind her ears, a movement so familiar to me it was almost instinctive.

I closed my eyes—determined not to see—turned my face to the snow, and felt the flakes land and melt with my tears.

Blossom's nose was warm and soft on my hand. "Blossom, we tried ... it was not enough."

I thought of Boomer—leaping high, his head arched like a mythological unicorn soaring —young and full of life.

Heaven blessed.

★ ★ ★

Falling snow carries a tinge of loneliness with it.

The house looked warm and cozy, every angle cuddled by an overlay of snow. Tendrils of smoke spiraled from the chimney, and comforting nutty-wood aromas from the fireplace reached me standing there.

Blossom's ears swiveled toward the woods.

"Aehh ..."

With sadness beyond my grasp, my heart cried out, *Don't go!*

Just beyond the stone wall, she stopped and turned her head over her shoulder. An elegant tawny doe, with a collar of ribbons encircling her neck as a talisman ...

Waiting.

MY JOURNEY

I walk the night by firefly light.
Tiny lanterns show the way, while
barn owls hoot and tree frogs sing
their songs to bring the day.

The road ahead leads to other towns
and places with other names
that lie beyond the mountains
across the distant plains.

It does not matter where I go
the end is not my goal.
My only wish, each footfall
leads me to my soul.

When my journeys over,
and my body is put to rest
place me near an oak tree
beneath a sparrow's nest,
for
Nature is my mother, and the sky
my father too. I'll find a
home in the palette of
earth's green and heaven's blue.

—JEANNE HAMILTON TROAST

Chapter 36

Author's Note

Robbed of one young buck named Boomer, Nature seemed more fragile, a little more degraded.

With a sense of urgency, Blossom snorted steamy breaths into the icy air and swung her head toward her den. She pawed the snow, anxious, her body language demanding, *"Follow me."*

There was no time to go back. I trudged into the thick blanket of snow.

Blossom's twiggy den, flecked with light and comforting muffled tones, always provided respite and a sweet sense of belonging. Halfway up the hill, I choked out a call.

"Boomer!"

As if she too anticipated Boomer would prance back into our lives, Blossom's front foot raised, ears pricking forward—only to droop as wispy snow-ghosts flitted here and there when the wind changed direction.

Later, with Blossom curled softly near the entrance, her head resting in my lap, she sighed. We gazed at everything but nothing in particular.

"Want some?" Blossom nibbled at my granola bar.

Although comforted by her crunching sounds, the nose bump of affection, my temples pounded with anger, and persistent worry overrode grief.

Would Blossom be next?

My resolve to stand up for humane animal rights was strong, unhindered by fear. I would not allow Blossom to become a pawn in somebody else's game. We would continue to open minds, hopefully touch a few more hearts, and empower advocacy to stop deliberate cruelty.

Too often in rural communities such as Tewksbury, a bulldozer changes the landscape and disrupts wildlife habitat. Another new road erodes a stream bank, and a tree, older than most of us, is gone forever.

From time to time, something extraordinary happens—something so wondrous that it becomes believable only while the experience is playing itself out. We certainly could not have foreseen the bit of fluff so close to death would grow into a lovely doe with a dazzling personality. We waited for the time she would choose her "wild side" and not look back at her human family. It never happened.

Blossom taught me to enjoy all that Nature offered. Importantly, her life made it clear that no fence, no collar or door, can stop an animal or person from leaving, either emotionally or physically, from a place they don't want to be. The cage of confinement ultimately makes the prize not worth the trouble.

Blossom died naturally in her sleep. She was ten. We buried her with a circle of flowers on her head, under the maple tree where she often rested.

I miss my 'wild' friend, our adventures—the next thrill waiting right outside the window —just beyond the door.

—Anna Carner

EPILOGUE

Reflecting on the extraordinary adventures I shared with Blossom over the decade, alongside the unforgettable moments with Baby Boomer and Buckaroo, I am deeply moved by the profound impact these gentle beings had on my life. Our bond was rooted in love and trust—a connection that I believe is fundamental in how we approach life and wildlife conservation.

Once, my son Glen playfully teased me after I stumbled over a lead line in the pasture, joking, "Hey, Mom, walk much or just read about it?" His words, though light-hearted, spurred me to move beyond mere reading—and to seek meaningful solutions.

In today's world, where empathy can sometimes be overshadowed by profit, the allure of a blue ribbon and a pat on the back may dull our sensitivity to the suffering of others and the essence of life in its purest form. I implore hunters to pause—take a moment to see the beauty and envision the love—before pulling the trigger.

Yet, amidst these challenges, there is hope. Technologies like SpayVac-for-Wildlife, a fertility-control vaccine, offer a promising and ethical alternative to mass slaughter. As deer face earlier and indiscriminate targeting, including pregnant does and fawns, it is crucial to reevaluate our relationship with these precious creatures of the wild and recognize their intrinsic value beyond mere population control. Humane deer population management can and should become the standard practice.

I urge you, dear Readers, to pause before making decisions that impact their lives. And please, remember Blossom, Boomer,

and Buckaroo—the love and joy they brought into our lives, and the potential for similar connections in your own.
　—Anna Carner

SpayVac-For-Wildlife

The mission of SpayVac-for-Wildlife Inc. is immunocontraception for overabundant wildlife. SpayVac is a pZP vaccine that has been proven to provide long-term birth control with a single injection in wild horses, macaques, deer, seals, and elephants.

It is my hope that one day soon, SpayVac® fertility control for wildlife will gain acceptance as a humane alternative to cruel and unnecessary slaughter.

PHOTOGRAPHS

Unicorn Hollow

Blossom kisses with Anna

Anna and Blossom as a fawn

Anna riding her horse, Justinian

The barn at Unicorn Hollow

Little girls: twins, Anna and Mary

Nurse Kuhn

Blossom and Kaya

Blossom nestled in hostas

Blossom on the patio

Pino and Blossom

Please Don't Shoot Blossom

Blossom in the News

Walking the horses

Winter on the farm

A hunter

Renfru

Bow-and-arrow hunting

Hunting Stand

DC in the spring

Mother and baby

Baby Boomer

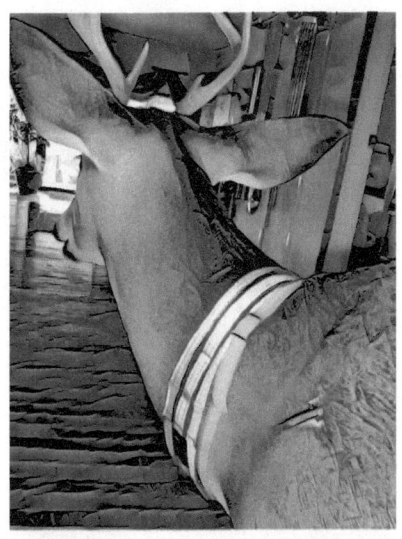

Hunter's arrow that got Boomer

Dr. Mike's miracle surgery

Blossom's love

A tribute

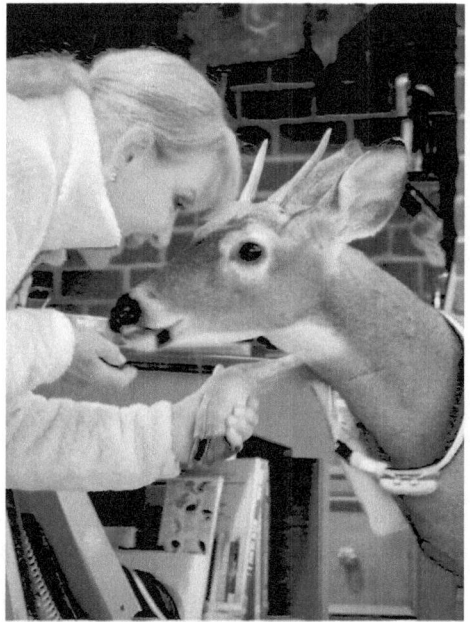

Friends for life

ABOUT THE AUTHOR

As one of the first women paramedics in Florida, Anna volunteered with several Fire Rescue squads during the tumultuous Cuban Mariel boatlift exodus and Miami riots in the '70s.

The Bahamas were only a day away, by boat. Several years of sailboat living, home-schooling her son, scuba diving, and exploring the island chain, were interspersed with true emergencies—where her medical training proved crucial to people living in the remote outer islands.

When Anna, her husband Pino, and a menagerie of animals moved to the community of nature-loving enthusiasts in Tewksbury, New Jersey, raising alpacas and competitive endurance trail riding became Anna's passions which continues on the current farm home in The Plains, VA.

Blossom, the wild fawn Anna rescued—a real-life Bambi— became a star in National Geographic's "Private Life of Deer" documentary. An editor asked her to write their story. It took years to complete *Blossom: The Wild Ambassador of Tewksbury*.

Anna continues to write while marketing the product brands she developed: Leather Therapy, Unicorn Fibre, and Unicorn Baby.

ACKNOWLEDGMENTS

Following the YouTube video "Pet Deer Blossom" and a call from Pangolin Pictures in NYC, Blossom became a star in the National Geographic documentary "The Private Life of Deer" for the PBS Nature channel.

I received a call from Georgia Hughes, a California bookseller. "Do you have the book? If not, write it!"

Blossom deserved her story to be told. After all, how difficult could it be to write a book? I know how to tell our story, right?

Wrong! It took years.

I am pleased to acknowledge the people in the writer's critique groups who helped make my dream a reality:

Angelle Bascom is a drama therapist with a mind full of stories. Mary Follin writes alternative reality adventures for the middle-grade category. Theresa Murphy is a physicist with a penchant for sci-fi. While I plodded through my manuscript, Chris Boswell wrote two full-length novels, Ron Moorefield edited his metaphysical trilogy, and Mike Durney shared his wit and self-published four books.

To my husband, Pino, for his love and support and for serving as my first line of defense against the dreaded first drafts. To my twin sister, Mary Forte, who read and challenged me to pull myself up by the bootstraps when writer's block threatened halfway through this book. For the guidance of Talia Carner, P.J. Fetner and the relentless enthusiasm from "the kids" in my family: Glen, Melanie, and Michael.

I want to extend heartfelt thanks to my consistently upbeat agent, Anna Termine, for her unwavering guidance and steadfast belief in the humanitarian impact of Blossom's story. Her dedication and support have been invaluable. A movie based on Blossom would be a testament to her support and an exciting new chapter in this journey.

WITH GRATITUDE

To my friend Jeanne Hamilton Troast for allowing me to share her inspiring poems within these pages. Jeanne experienced Blossom's magic up close and personal, translating her emotions and observations of nature, wildlife, and humanity into beautiful verse.

Jeanne, the eldest of three girls, was born into a military family and spent her childhood moving between Naval Air Stations across the United States. Her love for America's diverse people led her to pursue a degree in anthropology and photojournalism at Douglas College.

Awarded a scholarship by Rutgers, Jeanne traveled through New Jersey's farmlands as a photojournalist, specializing in written ethnographies of the communities she encountered.

In later years, she documented the various sports of her hometown, Tewksbury, New Jersey. Her photos are featured in "The History Of The Essex Fox Hounds."

Jeanne's love for horses and the diverse creatures around her farm developed her keen awareness of the importance of all living beings, human and animal alike. The poems in her book, "Songs of Life In The Key Of G," reflect her sensitivity to all living things.

Jeanne now resides in Tryon, N.C., beneath the beauty of the Blue Ridge Mountains.

I also want to acknowledge Mark Fraker for his research on SpayVac—a more humane contraceptive alternative to hunting to cull wildlife.

And, particularly, for the kindness and skill of Dr. Mike Fugaro who worked so hard to save our young buck, Baby Boomer. There are not enough words to convey my heartfelt thanks.

Sibylline Press is proud to publish the brilliant work of women authors over 50. We are a woman-owned publishing company and, like our authors, represent women of a certain age.

www.ingramcontent.com/pod-product-compliance
Lightning Source LLC
Chambersburg PA
CBHW021215130626
46554CB00004B/1234